Alphabet Puppets

Songs, Stories, and Cooking Activities
for Letter Recognition and Sounds

Jill M. Coudron

FEARON PITMAN PUBLISHERS, INC.

BELMONT, CALIFORNIA

This book is dedicated to the teachers,
student teachers, parents, and especially
the children at the St. Joseph Lab School,
for whom it was created

Edited by Margaret Cross *and* Carol Whiteley
Design by Rick Chafian
Illustrations by Jil! Coudron *and* Mary Burkhardt
Cover design by Dennis Ziemenski

Copyright © 1979 by Fearon Pitman
Publishers, Inc., 6 Davis Drive, Belmont,
California 94002. Member of the Pitman Group.
All rights reserved. No part of this book may
be reproduced by any means, transmitted, or
translated into a machine language without
written permission from the publisher.

ISBN-0-8224-0298-X
Library of Congress Catalog Card Number: 78-72077

Printed in the United States of America.

1.9 8 7 6 5 4 3 2 1

Contents

Introduction

The idea for the alphabet puppet program came with the realization and understanding that children come to school with many different levels of experience. We have children entering our schools who have traveled extensively, have watched educational television programs, and have gone to nursery schools. We also have children who have had little or no exposure to academic learning of any kind. How can we meet the needs of all these children in one classroom? The puppet program described in this book offers one way. It is fun and exciting, and the children's activities are varied and interesting. The program has value for all children, since it can enhance the experiences they have already had or use those experiences as starting points in new learning endeavors. No groupings are suggested which might make some children feel that they are better or worse than others. Since each week's program can be very different, it is not monotonous. Children are involved with the puppet and its story, song, and activities and, finally, with the cooking experience. Children learn when they *do*; they learn when they are *involved*; they learn when they *meet and get to know* people and animals, such as those the puppets in this program represent.

You will find as you read and experiment with the activities that specific objectives are often stated for each one. A number of general objectives are being met by the program as well:

- To increase awareness of self and to develop positive self-concepts.
- To develop imagination and creativity.
- To increase awareness of the names and sounds of letters.

1

- To perform activities that will develop and strengthen small- and large-muscle coordination.
- To develop skills in sequencing and memory building.
- To develop awareness of similarities and differences.
- To develop awareness of colors, shapes, and sizes.
- To develop listening and speaking skills.
- To offer children the opportunity to express themselves through dramatization and movement.
- To offer children the opportunity to express themselves artistically using paper, paint, crayons, clay, glue, play-dough, and other familiar materials.
- To involve parents in their children's education through discussion, collection of materials, and classroom reinforcement.

HOW THE PROGRAM WORKS

This alphabet program uses a letter-a-week approach. Short weeks can be used for review of letters already introduced or a letter you feel the children could experience in a few days. The letter from the previous week could also be extended into a following short week.

On Monday, introduce the puppet. It will be exciting for the children if you keep the puppet hidden in a special box until you are ready to present it. After a few weeks you can use the time before bringing out the new puppet to review the letters you have already worked with and let the children guess what the new letter may be. Once the children guess the letter, let them guess who the puppet might be; this activity should stimulate their thinking about the sound of that letter. Have the children close their eyes while you pull the puppet out of the box. They will be delighted when they uncover their eyes and see the new creature they will be learning about. Let them say hello to the puppet and touch it if they want to.

Next, let the puppet tell its story, which is stated at the beginning of each letter's activities. Speaking either as the puppet or as teacher, you can then ask the children to think of things the puppet may like to eat or other things relating to its letter. The puppet can tell each child his or her name in *puppet talk*, or in the *language of the letter*; that is, if the child's name is *Susie*, in *B* language the name will become *Busie*. Children are fascinated by this change. Find all the children who are *cousins* to the puppet (whose first or last name begins with its letter). These children can have special recognition during the alphabet time that week.

After these discussions, teach the children the song that accompanies the letter and try to get the children as involved as possible. All the songs have actions. Use these, and add any other movements you can think of. Do the actions with the children and enjoy yourself! At the end of the lesson, put the puppet on a special table. This table will become a gathering place where the children can play with the puppet and bring articles from home that begin with the puppet's letter. (The bringing of articles from home is an important way for children to involve their parents.)

Spend Tuesday, Wednesday, and Thursday doing the activities for the letter, relating each activity to the puppet. For example, you can say that the puppet has written a note to the children telling them the activities they are going to do that day. Or you can pretend that the puppet is whispering something in your ear for you to repeat to the children. It is essential that the children understand that the activities they do are to help them learn that week's letter and its sound. Besides doing the activities, review the story and sing the song each day. By the end of the week the children will know the song well and sing it enthusiastically.

Try to write a great deal as you work with the program. Write the names of the puppets on the chalkboard. Write a description of any activity you are beginning (for example, "We are blowing bubbles"). Let the children see printed words whenever possible and relate them to the letter and the activity. Children who are ready to read will probably be able to learn and remember words you have worked with during the week. Also have the children verbalize as much as possible. When they play hunting games, have relays, and do other activities, encourage them to say the name of the letter they are working with. Have them call out during a treasure hunt. Have them say the letter that is being passed to the next runner in a relay. This kind of activity is especially important for the child who has not been exposed to letter names. It is also invaluable reinforcement to those who have.

Friday—the culmination of the week's singing, games, activities, and learning—will be a special day if you choose to do the cooking then. Along with the cooking, list all the things the children have done that week, letting the class try to recall what was done each day. This recalling is excellent for memory building. Friday can also be a time for the children to talk about what they liked or did not like about the puppet and the activities. They are sure to like some things more than others—give them a chance to say so. By voicing their opinions they will begin to learn to judge, to develop critical thinking, and to listen to each other and respect each others' opinions.

CHARTING PROGRESS

How will you know what the children are learning in the alphabet program? Many aspects of their learning—such as listening and speaking skills and enthusiasm—you won't be able to evaluate concretely. But for letter and sound recognition, you can keep track of progress simply by using a chart like the one on page 4.

NAME																										
Recognition	A	B	C	D	E	F	G	H	I	J	K	L	M	N	O	P	Q	R	S	T	U	V	W	X	Y	Z
Recognition	a	b	c	d	e	f	g	h	i	j	k	l	m	n	o	p	q	r	s	t	u	v	w	x	y	z
Matching																										
Sounds																										

At the beginning of the year, sit down with each child and see what letters and sounds he or she knows. See who is able to match letters. Show the children some simple words to see if they can read them by recognizing the letters and sounds. Color in the boxes for the things each child knows. Periodically retest the children using a different recording color each time, so you can tell at a glance when the children learned what. This chart is an excellent means of showing parents their children's progress. The children will like the tracking chart, too, because they can understand it and see their progress, and they're thrilled to see their boxes colored in as they master new skills. Children are proud to share their accomplishments with their parents, and I often send a note home if a child shows mastery of several letters at one testing period.

INVOLVING PARENTS

You can involve the parents of the children in your classrooms in the alphabet program in a variety of ways. Most parents will be very enthusiastic about the puppets and will be happy to be part of the program. Sending parent letters home with the children each week to introduce the puppet of the week and list the activities you did will reinforce the learning—and the parents' interest. The parents can talk to their children about these activities, and if you put the songs and stories into the letters too, the parents can sing along with the children and listen knowledgeably to them as they tell the stories. (See Appendix A for a sample letter.)

Another way of getting parents involved is to invite them to school occasionally for a program. Have the children present several puppet stories through dramatizations and songs. Serve a snack that the children have helped to prepare during an alphabet cooking activity. Once I had the moms and dads come in during *V* Week and we shared our Vanilla Vudding. The parents were delighted! Parents may also be invited to play games during the program—the children love to see their parents playing, and parents have fun too.

You can also request that parents act as aides or assistants for special classroom projects or during field trips. A parent can find out what his or her child is doing at school in no better way than to be there. Parents are especially helpful on cooking day when you really need extra hands. If parents are willing to volunteer as aides on a permanent basis, by all means recruit them, and enjoy their assistance. They can be trained at the beginning of the year and will become an invaluable source of help.

Even if many parents can't help in the classroom, they can still encourage their children by talking to them about the letter of the week and asking about the day's activities. Helping their children find things to take to school for the puppet table keeps parents involved too.

Specific suggestions for involving parents are made throughout this book.

Making Alphabet Puppets

You are ready to begin the creation of your own set of alphabet puppets, which introduce and reinforce the letters of the alphabet for your children. Puppet patterns and specific directions for assembling them are included in Appendix B. The puppets can be made in a number of ways; choose one that seems most suitable to your available time and talents. Making the puppets is a big task but one that will bring much joy and satisfaction.

This chapter lists many ideas for making the puppets and what materials to use. As each puppet and alphabet letter is introduced in this book, you will find simple drawings which may suggest construction and decoration ideas to you—but use your own imagination to bring the puppets to life as you design and decorate them. The puppets don't have to be elaborate; a simple character can be very effective. Remember, the puppet is only the beginning. The rest is up to you!

Let the character of each puppet come alive at your fingertips. Try to feel the puppet's personality. Your enthusiasm is an important part of the puppet program. If you enjoy the activities, your children will too, and the program will be a happy success for everyone—and one in which the children are sure to learn. Your efforts will be rewarded as you lead your children into a world of fantasy, fun, and learning.

The patterns in Appendix B will guide you in constructing hand puppets of three basic designs. The puppets can be sewn or glued together. Sewing will produce a sturdier puppet that will last longer in the hands of eager children. Gluing will work well for the shorter term. Features can be either glued or sewn on.

MATERIALS

The puppets can be made from a variety of materials: felt, fake fur, knits, terrycloth, Pellon, cotton, or many other interesting textures. Heavier materials work best and stand up under pressure. Color choices are up to you, but do utilize colors that will help you teach the puppet's letter. For example, use blue, black, or brown for *B*, orange for *O*, red for *R*, and so on. Features should be cut from nonfraying materials like felt, Pellon, or knits. Features and decorations can also be cut from iron-on patches and ironed onto the puppet. Iron-on materials come in a wide variety of colors. The puppets will become more lifelike if you add real items such as a string of beads for B. B. Bunny, a hanky for Happy Hippo, a wig for Wacky Walrus, a cap for Curly Caterpillar, lace for Looney Lion, a zipper for Zippy Zebra, or a red ribbon with a ring for Racing Raccoon.

FEATURES

Some suggestions of materials to use for your puppets' features are listed below:

- *Eyes.* Commercial glue-on or sew-on eyes; commercial protruding-type eyes (good for puppets made of thick or furry materials).
- *Nose and Mouth.* Felt; iron-ons; knits.
- *Horns and Ears.* Double thickness of felt; knits. Pellon or cardboard can be used for reinforcing.
- *Legs and Feet.* Single thickness of cut-out felt, which can be sewn double and stuffed with nylon stockings or foam. Both Jolly Jogger and Kicky Kangaroo have a more realistic look with three-dimensional legs. Enor Elephant's trunk can also be made in this way.
- *Hair or Manes.* Cut-up wigs; various plys of yarn (fat yarn used for wrapping packages can be pulled apart and separated into thin strips to get a curly effect); fake furs; other materials cut into fine strips.
- *Whiskers.* Commercial whiskers; cut felt; knits.
- *Tails.* Long pieces of yarn or felt; braided yarn.
- *Letters.* Each puppet has both the upper- and lower-case letter attached to its body. These letters can be made from felt or other fabrics.
- *Hats and Caps.* Felt or knits attached in a single thickness; two-dimensional hats from double thicknesses sewn or glued together; ends of socks, custom-knit or crocheted variety.
- *Specific Features.* For features that deal with a specific letter, use felt or a similar material. For example, you can cut out a felt pumpkin for Polka

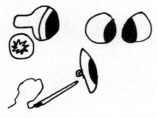

Eyes

Nose, mouth, horns, ears

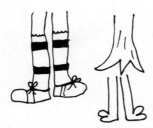

Legs and feet

Hair or manes

Letters

Hats and caps

Finger puppet

Sack puppet

Paper character

Paper-cup puppet

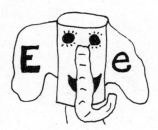

Paper-tube puppet

Kitchen utensil puppets

Old-sock, mitten puppets

Box puppets

Pig, a felt heart for Happy Hippo, or a felt leaf for Looney Lion. Felt-tip marking pens can be used for adding details like freckles, spots, stripes, feathers, or the like. If the color wears off, add more. Pipe cleaners, sewn between thin strips of material, can be added to ears, legs, trunks, tails, and antennae, lending flexibility. Ugboo's antennae are much more realistic when they wind around—with pipe cleaners inside whatever fabric you choose. Wiggly Worm's body, B. B. Bunny's ears, and Enor's trunk will work well with pipe-cleaner reinforcement.

ALTERNATIVES TO HAND PUPPETS

- *Finger Puppets.* Finger puppets are made from material or paper scraps. Attach them to your finger with a ring of heavy paper. Fingers from old gloves will work.

- *Sack Puppets.* Use lunch or bakery sacks for the body of these puppets, drawing, painting, or gluing on features. The sacks can be stuffed and tied.

- *Paper Characters.* Draw or paint these characters in a variety of sizes on heavy paper such as tagboard. Cut out the drawings and mount them on sticks, pencils, or rulers. Arms and legs, as well as heads, can be attached to the main body with brass fasteners to give the characters more mobility. Laminate these characters to help them withstand wear.

- *Paper-Cup Puppets.* Small paper cups are used as the base for these puppets. Your thumb and a finger, emerging through holes cut in the sides of the cup, act as arms. The puppets can also be held by ice cream sticks taped to the inside of the cup with designs and body parts drawn on.

- *Paper-Tube Puppets.* Cut tubing from wrapping and other papers into sections and decorate them for use as bases for the puppets. Features can be glued, painted, or drawn on.

- *Kitchen Utensil Puppets.* Use spatulas, wooden spoons, or strainers for the faces of these puppets. Make the faces removable so you won't need many utensils to create a number of characters. You can tape the faces on or make them double so that they can be slipped over the utensil.

- *Old-Sock Puppets or Mitten Puppets.* Use these materials as bases for bodies. Sew or glue on features.

- *Box Puppets.* Cover and decorate small shoeboxes, milk cartons, cereal boxes, and other varieties of boxes for use as puppet characters.

Things to Do with All the Puppets

GENERAL ACTIVITIES

Listed in the following pages are general activities, songs, and stories which may be used with any or all of the puppets (in addition to the specific activities listed for each letter). You will want to refer to this section of the book as you work with each puppet. Choose those activities which appeal to you and your children. Generally, choosing one activity (or two brief activities) for each day will work best. If you plan to devote extra time to the program, you could use more activities, as they do encompass all curriculum areas. You may also wish to use some of the group and individual games described in the chapter entitled "Alphabet Week."

- *Letter Hunt.* Hide several pieces of paper with a given letter written on each. Tell the children to try to find as many of the papers as possible, calling out "I found a (name of letter)" when they are successful. When the hunt is finished, have the children count the number of letters they found. (This activity incorporates another skill—counting—into the alphabet program.)
- *Human Letter.* Have the children use their bodies to make letters. They can create the shapes in a standing position, but it is also fun to lie down on the floor to make them. Have the children work in pairs or teams. It is great fun, too, for the whole class to make one large letter, if you have the space.
- *Newspaper Letter Cutting.* Finding and cutting out specific letters in the newspaper will help the children learn the letters. Use only common

letters (*S, T, B, M*, for example) for this activity—many young children get discouraged easily if a task is too difficult.

- *Listening Game.* Say words to the children and have them listen for those that begin with a certain letter. Ask them to respond in some way pertinent to the letter; for example, if they are listening for the *S* sound, they might hiss when they hear *S* words.

- *Drawing the Puppet and Its Story.* The children can make and take home drawings related to the week's story and retell it to parents or siblings.

- *Tactile Letter Experience.* Draw the letters on paper and have the children add some kind of material over the lines. For example, children could glue beans over the lines of a *B*, rice over the lines of an *R*, or cotton over the lines of a *C*.

- *Work Sheets.* Prepare work sheets on which the children must identify and circle pictures of items that begin with a given sound or letter.

- *Cutting Out Pictures for a Sound.* Have the children search through old magazines and catalogs to find items that begin with a given letter or sound.

- *Treasure Hunts.* Draw a different clue for each child. You may conduct the hunt in two ways. Hide a treasure that begins with the letter under study. Write a child's name on each clue. Then hide all the clues but one. Give the first clue to the child whose name is on it. It will lead the child to a second clue with another child's name on it, and so on, until the last clue leads to the treasure. Or you may hide a small item at each location and pass out all the clues at once, so that each child is led to a treasure. Since very few children will be able to read, the picture clues allow everyone to take part in the hunt. As the year progresses, you may wish to add simple words to the clues along with the drawing of the object: "Go to the _____." Each child can share his or her clue with parents at home and explain the hunt.

- *Song.* Use a simple song, such as "Old MacDonald Had a Farm," and put in the letter you are working on:

Old MacDonald had a farm, ee-ai-ee-ai-o,
And on his farm he had a (name of letter), ee-ai-ee-ai-o.
With a (make sound of letter twice) here and a (sound, twice) there,
Here a (sound), there a (sound), everywhere a (sound, twice). . . .

- *Dramatization.* Let the children act out the puppet stories. Acting is a good way for children to express themselves; it is also a good way to practice the sequencing skill, getting the events of the stories in correct order.

- *Parent Involvement.* Invite the children's parents to school often. Have the class dramatize the puppet stories, sing the songs, and play alphabet games with their parents. Let children prepare a simple recipe to share.

- *Talking in the Language of the Puppet. Puppet talk* is a good way to work with letter sounds. For example, if you want the puppet to say "Good morning, children" in *Z* language, it would sound like this: "Zood zorning, zhildren." It sounds silly, but children love the challenge of figuring out what is being said and will enthusiastically respond in the same manner. You can say simple sentences in the language of the letter and have the children translate.

- *Learning to Write the Letter.* Appendix C gives directions for teaching letter formation. This skill can be taught on one day each week, along with the other activities.

- *Thinking of Things That Begin with the Letter.* Have the children brainstorm and name all the objects they can think of that begin with a given letter and write down the names of the objects in word or picture form.

- *Finding a Letter.* Scatter different letters across the chalkboard or chart paper. Repeat the letter being studied enough times so that many or all of your children can find and circle one. The children can take turns searching for the letter of the week.

- *Bringing Things from Home.* Each week, encourage the children to bring things from home for the puppet table. Let the children tell about their treasures at a sharing time, if you want. Otherwise, have the children put the objects on a puppet table to work with during their free time.

THE COOKING EXPERIENCE

Cooking is a new and exciting adventure for many children. So let them be as involved in it as possible. Let the children measure, pour, stir, shake, read the recipe, clean up, and eat! The more they are able to do, the more meaningful the experience will be for them. Your open attitude and encouragement will help them gain confidence in their abilities, and this confidence will carry over into their homes. Parents have often told me how surprised they were that their children were more willing to help in the kitchen after they began cooking in school.

You may wish to create a kitchen corner in the classroom. Keep it stocked with general supplies you'll use in many projects, including:

salt	plastic eating utensils
pepper	(include knives for cutting)
flour	parer
sugar	sifter
cooking oil	egg beater
large wooden mixing spoons	spatula
measuring cup and spoons	strainer
mixing bowls	pastry brush
baking pans	paper plates
small serving bowls	paper cups
toothpicks	paper towels

If space does not allow for a kitchen corner, be sure to read each recipe carefully on the day before a cooking activity so that you can assemble all necessary ingredients and utensils.

Your preparation for the cooking activities is most important. Think through each step, and plan the equipment and procedure to use with your group. Write the recipe clearly on a large chart or the chalkboard (with illustrations or symbols, if you wish). Sometimes you may want to cook with the entire group. At other times you may want to break the experience into activities for small groups: one group could do the planning, one the shopping, one the mixing, one the cooking, and, finally, one the cleaning up. As you go through the year, vary the approach you use, and try different strategies with different recipes.

The recipes have been chosen for their natural, nutritious ingredients and their simplicity. Each letter's recipe(s) can be cooked in the classroom without benefit of stove or oven. A few recipes require access to a refrigerator. If you can obtain a corn popper, an electric skillet, and a hot plate, you will be able to handle all the cooking. Recipes are included for meat dishes, vegetables, fruits, drinks, and some treats are included. The recipes are intended to serve small portions to 20 to 24 children, but they can be easily adapted to suit larger or smaller groups.

Exposing children to healthful foods and allowing them to share in their preparation is a first step toward teaching them how to eat well. If the children prepare these recipes again at home, their parents may be encouraged to provide better nutrition for the family.

The rewards of the cooking period are the joy of doing and the joy of eating. Some children may be apprehensive about trying new and different foods, but encourage them to do so. If children participate in the creation of foods, they are more likely to taste them. The cooks in the school where this program was used commented that they could really tell that the children had been cooking in kindergarten—children were much easier to please and more willing to try the foods prepared for them.

Introducing the Consonants

B. B. Bunny

Use Patterns 1 and 4.

STORY

My name is B. B. Bunny. I live under a blackberry bush in the barnyard. I eat lots of bread, beans, bananas, and berries. B. B. is my nickname—it's short for *Basketball*. I love to play basketball more than anything else. I am very good at bouncing the ball and making baskets. I play with the Bunny Basketball Team. We play the beavers, the bears, and the baboons. We always beat them. We play with a big, brown basketball we found in a barn.

SONG
(tune of "Battle Hymn of the Republic," chorus only)

Little B. B. Bunny likes to bounce a basketball,
Little B. B. Bunny likes to bounce a basketball,
Little B. B. Bunny likes to bounce a basketball,
A big, brown basketball.

ACTIONS

bunny: make ears above head with hands
basketball: make a circle with hands

19

bounce: pretend to bounce a ball
big: hold arms outstretched
(*How to use the song:* First, sing the entire song and do the accompanying actions. Second, sing the entire song but don't sing the word *bunny* when it appears; just do the action for that word. Third, sing the song omitting the words *bunny* and *basketball,* but use the actions for those words. Fourth, omit the words *bunny, basketball,* and *bounce,* using the actions instead. Fifth, omit *bunny, basketball, bounce,* and *big,* and substitute the actions for all four words.)

ACTIVITIES

- Mix some liquid detergent and water in a bowl. Give each child a pipe cleaner to bend into a bubble wand—a loop with a handle. Have a few children at a time dip their wands into the bubbles. The rest of the class can watch or try to catch the bubbles. This activity is a good one to do outdoors.

- Clip several letter *B*s out of old magazines and newspapers. The children can then cut out big circles of blue or black construction paper and glue the *B*s on these circles. Children can also make *B* Banners by gluing *B*s on large blue or brown rectangles to hang like flags in the classroom.

- The class can play Boo. Have the children line up on a preselected goal line. Choose one child to be Boo. Have Boo go to another designated goal line and pretend to be asleep. The rest of the class should walk toward Boo, chanting "Starlight, moonlight, Boo will not be out tonight." When the children get close to Boo, he or she should shout "Boo!" and try to tag a child before everyone crosses the line. The tagged child becomes Boo next, and the game continues.

- The class can play Bell Ball. Ask all the children except one to sit in a circle and pass around a ball. Have the selected child, without looking at the circle, ring a bell at intervals. Whoever is holding the ball when the bell rings leaves the circle. The game continues until only one child is left. That child is bell ringer for the next game.

- Have a balloon-breaking relay. Divide the children into teams and place a chair for each team on a goal line 8 or 9 feet from the starting line. To play, one child from each team runs to the team's chair, sits on an inflated balloon to break it, and returns to the group at the starting point. The team that first breaks all its balloons wins.

- The class can make birds out of balloons. Each child will need one balloon, papier-mâché materials, art paper, and paint. First, have the children cover the balloons with the papier-mâché. Let the balloons dry completely. Then paint the covered balloons and let them dry again. Have each child cut out wings, a head, and a tail and glue them onto the balloon body. Legs made from pipe cleaners can be added. Hang the birds from the ceiling or light fixtures.

- Big, beautiful bugs that are black, blue, and brown can be painted on art paper.
- An unusual activity involves bending a bone. Soak a large, clean, unbroken chicken bone in a glass of vinegar for at least 12 hours. The acid in the vinegar will dissolve the calcium in the bone, allowing you to bend it. If it is long enough, let the children try to tie the bone in a knot.

COOKING

Butter

1/2 pint cream   1 big plastic jar with lid   salt   bread or crackers

Pour the cream into the jar and screw on the lid. Let each child shake the jar until the cream turns to butter. As the children shake the jar, have them chant: "Go, cream, go! Come, butter, come! Shake, shake, shake! Butter it will make." Pour off the liquid, and add a pinch of salt to the butter. Serve with bread or crackers.

Baked Bananas

(An optional activity if you have access to an oven)

bananas   lemon juice   sugar   salt

Provide 1/2 banana for each child. Preheat the oven to 375° F. Halve the bananas lengthwise. Bake them in their peels for about 20 minutes. Sprinkle the peeled bananas with lemon juice, sugar, and salt.

Curly Caterpillar

Use Pattern 3.

STORY

My name is Curly Caterpillar. I think I'm a cute caterpillar. I have curls all over my body. I comb them to keep them cute. But I am forever catching colds. It is so awful! With the cold comes an annoying cough that sounds like this: "C-C-C-C" (**hard C** sound). A friend made me a cap and a cape to wear to help me keep from catching more colds. When my colds get very bad, I cry.

SONG
(tune of "Skip to My Lou")

1. What can we do with our caterpillar?
   What can we do with our caterpillar?
   What can we do with our caterpillar
   Who has a cough and cold?
Chorus:
   Cough, cough, coughing Curly,
   Cough, cough, coughing Curly,
   Cough, cough, coughing Curly,
   Coughing, crying Curly.

2. Curly wears a cap and cape.
   Curly wears a cap and cape.
   Curly wears a cap and cape
   To keep from catching cold. (*Chorus*)
3. Curly likes to comb her curls,
   Curly likes to comb her curls,
   Curly likes to comb her curls,
   Cute, combing Curly. (*Chorus*)

ACTIONS

cough: cover mouth with hand
crying: make crying sound with voice when singing word
comb: pretend to comb body

ACTIVITIES

- Have the children draw a large letter *C* on a sheet of construction paper. They can use the *C* as the beginning of a picture, perhaps a face or a bug. Let them complete their pictures with crayons or colored markers.

- The children can play a game called Captain, May I? To begin, ask the children to stand in a line, facing you. Then give each child, one at a time, a direction, such as "Take one baby step forward." The child must say "Captain, may I?" in order to move. If the child forgets to say these words, he or she must go back to (or remain on) the beginning line. Other commands may include giant steps, scissor cuts (make one jump to land with feet wide apart, another to bring them together again), egg beaters (twirling-around jumps), jumps, hops, and so on. Vary the number of steps in each command. Also, tell the children they may try to move forward when you're not looking. If you don't see them, they get to stay in the new place. If they are caught, they must return to the starting line.

- Bring some modeling clay to the classroom. Ask the children to make anything, such as a cow or a cat, whose name begins with the letter *C*.

- Bring some crickets to your classroom in a jar. Have the students observe their activities. Then, get some books and pictures that tell about crickets, and share these facts with the children. A chart can be made to indicate what has been learned.

- Have a crawling contest. Divide the children into teams for a relay. One child from each team crawls at the same time. He or she must crawl to and from a predetermined spot, then tap the next runner and say "C" before the next child can crawl.

- Give the children large pieces of construction paper and have them cut out a caterpillar body, eyes, and antennae. Then, show the children how to cut strips of paper and curl them around a pencil. Have the class glue the curls, eyes, and antennae onto the body to make a friend for Curly Caterpillar. The caterpillars can be colored, too.

- Play a listening game. If the children hear a hard *C* word, they cough; if not, they remain quiet.

- Have the children cut out from magazines and catalogs pictures of things that begin with the letter *C*. Ask the class members, either alone or in groups, to make collages with the pictures.

- Tell the children they are going to make cardboard cars. Each child will need a piece of cardboard 4 or 5 inches square; this is the car body. To it the children can add windows, an antenna, or whatever features they want. Paper circles (wheels) can be glued on or attached with brass fasteners. The cars can be colored when completed.

- Have a Cap Day during *C* Week. Let the children wear caps and keep them on all day.

- Locate California and Canada (or other appropriate places beginning with *C*) on a map. Ask if anyone has been to one or more of these places. Discuss the climate in those areas.

- Let the class make cloud pictures. Cotton balls can be stretched and glued down to paper to make the clouds; the rest of the picture may be drawn in.

COOKING

Carrot Curls

peeled raw carrots   *large pan of ice water*   *toothpicks*

With a vegetable parer, shave lengthwise strips from the carrots. Let each child have a turn to try this (make sure they work carefully with the sharp implement). Show the class how to curl a strip around a finger and secure it with a toothpick. Place the curls in ice water until they're cold, and then drain them. Let each child have several.

Cocoa

1 c. hot milk   1 t. chocolate syrup

Provide the above ingredients for each child. Pour the milk into individual cups and let the children measure one teaspoon of syrup from a small container into their cups. Stir well and enjoy.

Ditto Dog

Use Patterns 1 and 10.

STORY

My name is Ditto Dog. I love dust and dirt. I play in them all the time. I am covered with dots, so people call me a dotty dog. I have a diamond and a daisy. Sometimes I act dizzy. When I am not playing in the dirt, I am doodling pictures. I live in a doghouse by the driveway. I like to dig in the dirt by my doghouse all day.

SONG
(tune of "Camptown Races")

Oh, Ditto is a dirty dog,
Dee dee, dee dee,
Ditto is a dirty dog,
Oh, dee dee day.
Chorus:
Ditto is a dog.
Ditto is a dog.
I'd give a dime
To dig with that dog.
Oh, dee dee day.

Other Verses
Substitute *dotty, dizzy, doodling, digging, doggone, D-D* for *dirty.*

ACTIONS

dog: make hands down from head like ears
dee (first and third): touch hands to head
dee (second and fourth): touch hands to shoulders
day: put hands on waist

Other Actions
Do appropriate actions for the words in the other verses.

ACTIVITIES

- Have the children draw crayon pictures or doodles (abstract designs) of things that begin with the letter *D.*
- Have the children draw giant *D*s on paper. Then ask them to decorate the *D*s with dots, drawing and coloring the dots or cutting out dots and gluing them on.
- The class can play the game Telephone, using messages that begin with the letter *D.* Sit with the children in a circle. Then you or a child should whisper a message that begins with *D* into the ear of the next child. Each child should continue to pass on the message he or she hears until the last person hears the message and says it out loud.
- Teach the children how to play dominoes. Hold a dominoes tournament.
- Bring some fresh white daisies to the classroom (or ask a child to bring some from the family garden). Put the flowers into containers of water with different food colorings. Watch the daisies change color.
- Have the class make denim pictures. Give each child a small piece of denim to glue to a piece of paper and draw a picture around. (The denim will form an element of the picture.)
- Teach the class to play Dog, Dog, Duck. Ask the children to sit in a circle and choose one to be It. Tell It to move around the circle tapping each child on the head, saying, "Dog," "Dog," "Dog," until he or she decides to say "Duck." The child who is named Duck must run around the circle and try to tag It before he or she reaches Duck's place. If Duck tags It, It must go to the center of the circle, which is the duck pond, and Duck becomes It. If It makes it safely to Duck's place, It continues for another round. The game continues until all the children have had a turn to be It.
- Teach the children a new dance. Have someone play a drum or tap out a beat during the dance.

- Make a dot-to-dot picture of something that begins with the letter *D*. Duplicate, and give one to each child. Explain to the children how they must connect the dots by following the numbers in the right order. Children can complete and color the picture.
- Show the class how to make play-dough. Mix 2 cups of flour, 1 cup of salt, 1 tablespoon of oil, and 1 cup of water. Knead well. Food coloring can be added with the water if desired. Give each child some play-dough to work with. Rolling pins to flatten the dough, cookie cutters for creating shapes, and plastic eating utensils for use in adding decorations make this project more interesting.
- Invite a dentist to come in and talk to the children.

- Have the children make paper dogs. Each child will need two large paper triangles, glue, crayons, and scissors. Tell the children to take one triangle and fold down two of the corners for ears, and fold one of the corners up for the nose. On the second triangle, have them fold one corner up for a tail and cut out a small square into the bottom edge for the legs. Then the children can glue the head to the body and decorate the dogs with dots, daisies, and diamonds.

COOKING

Ducks in the Duck Pond

bread   eggs   butter   salt   pepper

Provide one slice of bread and one egg for each child. Preheat an oven or an electric skillet at 325° F. and grease a large baking pan. Toast the slices of bread in the skillet (or a toaster, if one is available) and butter them. Then cut a circle in each slice of bread with a cookie cutter. Save the circles. Put the bread and the circles in the buttered baking pan. Break an egg into each hole. Salt and pepper the egg. Bake or heat 10–12 minutes. Cut the bread circles in half. Add the halves to the egg "ducks" to suggest wings.

Friendly Frog

Use Patterns 1 and 8.

STORY

My name is Friendly Frog. I am friendly with everyone and funny, too. I have a friend, Fancy Fish, who goes wherever I go. We are fantastic friends. I have many freckles, just like Fancy Fish. I have five fat spots on my front side and four fat spots on my back. Four and five are my favorite numbers. I live with a family on a farm where we all eat our favorite food—flapjacks—every morning. I like to flip-flop.

SONG
(tune of "London Bridge")

1. Friendly is a funny frog,
       funny frog, funny frog.
   Friendly is a funny frog.
   Flip-flop Friendly.
2. Friendly has a family,
       family, family.
   Friendly has a family,
   Flip-flop Friendly.

3. Friendly's friend is Fancy Fish,
   Fancy Fish, Fancy Fish.
   Friendly's friend is Fancy Fish.
   Flip-flop Friendly.
4. Friendly likes the letter F,
   letter F, letter F.
   Friendly likes the letter F.
   Flip-flop Friendly.
5. F F F F F F F,
   F F F, F F F.
   F F F F F F F,
   Flip-flop Friendly.

ACTIONS

funny: act goofy
flip-flop: flip-flop forward and back
family: hold up fingers
fish: make swimming motions
letter F: make an F with fingers—two fingers across, one finger up and down

ACTIVITIES

- Make some classroom fishing poles by tying a string around a stick and tying a magnet to the end of the string. The children can fish for cut-out letters, numbers, or Fs that have paper clips attached.

- Let the children make fingerprint Fs. First, set small dishes of tempera paint on tables. Have the children dip one finger into the paint and print it in the shape of an F on a sheet of paper. The children can print capital and small Fs and pictures of things that begin with F.

- Let the children paint with their feet. (This activity is a good one to do outdoors.) Work with only a few children at a time. Each child can take a turn putting paint on one foot of another child, who then tries to paint with that foot. You can have each of them put a footprint on a very large mural-type paper to hang in the classroom. Be sure to have a hose or buckets of water and towels for clean-up.

- Take the class to visit a fire station. Learn what firefighters do.

- Let the children paint freckles on each other to look more like Friendly. White tempera paint works well and comes off easily.

- For dramatic play, put on some music and let the children pretend to fly, act ferocious, flop, and use their feet in a variety of ways.

- Assemble a flower-arranging center for your classroom by gathering a number of artificial flowers and plastic vases (ask the children to bring some from home). Be sure to use only unbreakable vases or oatmeal boxes weighted with a little sand or clay. Children can make bouquets at the center in their free time. You may wish to tell other faculty members about the project and let them put in orders for the children to fill.

- Have the children make Fuzzies (yarn balls or pompoms) using yarn scraps brought from home. Each child will need yarn, scissors, a 3-inch square of cardboard, and construction paper for eyes and a mouth. Have the children wind lengths of yarn around the cardboard to build up thick sections. Have them carefully remove each wrapped section of yarn and tie the sections together in the center. Then have the children cut through the ends and fluff out the ball. Cut-out eyes and a mouth can be glued to the Fuzzies to give them faces.

- Teach the children a dance about friends called "Friend, Oh, Friend" (to the tune of "Brother Come and Dance with Me" from *Hansel and Gretel*). Begin the dance with one couple, and tell the class to keep singing and dancing until everyone has been chosen and is dancing.

SONG

Friend, oh, friend, how do you do?
Both my hands I give to you.
Round we go; round again.
Then I'll find another friend.

ACTIONS

how do you do?: shake hands
give: extend hands to partner
round: partners swirl in circle
find: each partner chooses another friend and repeats the dance

COOKING

Friendly's Fantastic Flapjacks

2 c. flour 1/2 t. salt 3 t. baking powder 1 T. honey
2 eggs 1-1/4 c. milk 1/4 c. oil butter
honey, jelly, or syrup topping

Sift the dry ingredients together. Beat the eggs and add the honey and milk. Combine the egg mixture with the dry ingredients. Add the oil. Then mix until smooth, but don't overmix. Pour batter in small amounts, in the shape of *F*s if desired, onto a griddle or electric skillet and brown on both sides. Top the flapjacks with butter and honey, jelly, or syrup. One recipe makes about three dozen small flapjacks.

Goofy Ghost

Use Pattern 2.

STORY

My name is Goofy Ghost. I'm goofy because I'm so different from other ghosts. I live in a green garbage can. I wear glasses. I play a guitar. And instead of saying "Oooooooo" or "Boo!" to scare people, I make a gargling sound like this—"G-G-G-G-G-G" (hard *G* sound)—and say "Goo!" Those noises scare people just as well! I love things that glitter and glow, and I have glittering letter *G*s all over me. My favorite colors are green and gold. Sometimes I wish I were a green ghost instead of a white one. I like to play the game of golf with my Grandmother.

SONG
(tune of "For He's a Jolly Good Fellow")

1. Oh, you're a goofy, good ghost.
   Oh, you're a goofy, good ghost.
   You're a goofy, good ghost.
   Goofy, Goofy Ghost.

Other Verses
Substitute *groovy*, *gargling*, *gleeful*, and *glittery* for *goofy*.

32

ACTIONS

you're: point to Goofy
goofy: make a silly face
ghost: make circles around eyes with fingers

Other Actions
Do actions that the words for the other verses indicate.

ACTIVITIES

- Play a guessing game with the children called I'm Thinking of Something, using words that begin with the sound of hard G. You might use such words as game, gate, gum, garden, gas, grass, green, garbage, golf, guitar, gloves, grasshopper, gorilla, and goldfish.

- Tell the class the story of Goldilocks. Talk about the possible reasons behind her name. Have the children draw a picture of Goldilocks, concentrating on her hair.

- Hold a G Relay. Divide the children into teams called the geese, the gorillas, the goats, and the grasshoppers. Then place one plastic or paper letter G on each of four places (chairs or tables) across the room. On the signal "Go," have the first child on each team run across the room, get a G, run back and give it to the next runner, saying "G." The next team member then runs and sets the G back on the original spot, and so on.

- Have the children create green ghosts with glasses. Using large sheets of green construction paper, let the children cut out eyes and mouths, draw on glasses, and decorate their ghosts with capital and small Gs.

- Show the children a globe. Talk about how it is different from a map. Find the area where your school is located and other points of interest.

- Grow grass in soil or a sponge in empty milk cartons by sprinkling seed in evenly and keeping it moist. You could also start a little garden in your room, using dishpans or any available containers for planters. A child's plastic swimming pool could house a larger gardening project.

- Teach the children how to gallop. Galloping to music is even more fun.

- Celebrate Grandparent's Day during G Week. Invite local grandparents in for a little program and treat.

- Have the children draw letter Gs with glue on sheets of paper. Then give each child a small paper cup with glitter in it, and let the children sprinkle glitter over the glue letters.

- Take the class to visit a gas station. Let the children watch how a gas tank is filled and how cars are hoisted up to be worked on.

COOKING

Goofy's Granola

4 c. rolled oats   2 c. wheat germ   1 c. chopped nuts
3/4 c. brown sugar   3/4 c. oil   1/3 c. water   2 T. vanilla
Optional: *1 c. sunflower seeds (hulled), 1 c. coconut, 1 c. raisins, milk*

Combine all the ingredients and mix well. Spread the mixture in a
15-by-10-by-1-inch jelly roll pan or two cake pans. Bake at 350° F. for about
an hour, stirring frequently. Cool the cereal, and add one cup of raisins,
sunflower seeds, or coconut if desired. Serve with or without milk. You can
vary granola ingredients to your taste without affecting the recipe. Granola is
good and nutritious and can be used in cakes, cookies, and breads. A variation of this recipe follows.

Goofy's Great Granola

4 c. rolled oats   1 c. wheat germ   1 c. honey or molasses   1 c. oil
1 c. chopped nuts   2 t. cinnamon   1/2 t. nutmeg
Optional: *sunflower seeds, sesame seeds, coconut, raisins*

Mix all the ingredients well. Cook the cereal in an electric skillet at about
325° F. for 10 to 15 minutes or until browned, stirring frequently. Cool, and
add one cup of raisins, sunflower or sesame seeds, or coconut if desired.

Happy Hippo

Use Patterns 1 and 7.

STORY

My name is Happy Hippo. I am very heavy, as most hippos are. I live with my other hippo friends in a house that's always hot. We sleep on heaps of hay. I have lots of hair, a hankie full of holes, several hats, and a big heart. My favorite game is Hide-and-Seek. I hide in a hut when it's my turn to hide. Listen to me laugh: "Ha, ha, ha, ha, ha!"

SONG
(tune of "Alouette")

1. Happy Hippo has a lot of hats.
   Happy Hippo has a lot of hats.
   Teacher: Hurrah for Happy and his hats.
   Children: Hurrah for Happy and his hats.
   Teacher: Happy's hats.
   Children: Happy's hats.
   All: Ho . . . Ho . . . Ho . . .

Other Verses
For *hats*, substitute *hair*, *heart*, and *holes*. Add the other words one verse at a time and repeat the previous verse, just as in the song "Alouette."

35

ACTIONS

hats: make hat with hands above head
hurrah: shake arms as though cheering

Other Actions
Do actions that the words for the other verses indicate.

ACTIVITIES

- Have the children make hats using construction paper, crayons, and glue.
- Open a center for your classroom called the Hat Shop for Happy. The children can use this center in their free time for dramatic play. Encourage the children to bring hats in from home, and set up a large mirror or two so the children can see themselves. Toy money and a cash register would complete the hat shop.
- Have each child choose a partner and lie on the floor to make capital and small *H*s with their bodies.
- Bring a hamster to school for a classroom pet (a child might bring his or her own to the class for a few days). Let the children observe the hamster's actions and habits.
- Have the class make hanger people. Each child will need two coat hangers taped together so that the rounded tops form a head and the triangular sections overlap crosswise to form the arms and legs. Each child will also need scissors, glue, and crayons. Tell the children to cut clothing out of paper for the hanger people along with faces, hats, shoes, and so on. Whatever is cut must be cut double (for a front and a back) and a little larger than the hanger so it will fit. When the objects are cut, show the children how to fit them around the hangers, and glue or staple the edges.
- Have a Hello Time. Ask the class to think of different ways people greet each other.
- Teach the children how to dance and sing the "Hokey-Pokey." Sing the song later using *H* things like head, hands, heart, hair.
- Show the children how to play Howdy, Partner. In the game one child is blindfolded and another child is It. It says, "Howdy, partner," in whatever kind of voice he or she chooses. The blindfolded child must try to guess who is talking.
- Ask the class to draw pictures of large holes on a sheet of paper and then draw in the holes pictures of things that begin with *H*. *H* pictures could also be cut out of magazines and glued onto the holes.
- Let the class experiment with hula hoops. Children can run, crawl, jump, and inchworm through them.

- Have a Hat Day during which the children wear hats they have made or brought from home. Prizes could be given for the most creative hats.
- Find someone who can play the harmonica, and ask him or her to play for the children.
- Have the class make horse tails out of yarn or paper. Then let them wear their tails by tying them around their waists or pinning them on. Play some music and let the children move to it as horses.

COOKING

Hurry-Ups 1

crackers or slices of bread   *2 T. peanut butter*   *1 T. raisins*

Provide the above ingredients for each child. Have the children mix the peanut butter with raisins and spread it on bread or crackers. If they don't wish to mix the two, the peanut butter could be spread on the bread and the raisins placed over it in the shape of an *H*.

Hurry-Ups 2

bananas   *wheat germ in a container for shaking*

Provide 1/2 banana for each child. Have the children slice or chunk their bananas. Then have them put the slices in the wheat germ container and shake it until the bananas are well coated. Tell the children to chant "Happy Hippo hurries to get hurry-ups" while they shake.

Jolly Jogger

Use Pattern 1.

STORY

My name is Jolly Jogger. I live in a jungle. I love to jog around the jungle. I jog every morning and every evening. Some people think I'm a jitterbug because I am always jogging, jumping, jostling, jiggling, and jerking. I also jabber a lot. I jabber about all kinds of junk like jewelry, jack-o'-lanterns, jellyfish, and jackets. I collect junk. My favorite food is Jell-O made from juice.

SONG
(tune of "London Bridge Is Falling Down")

1. Jog along with Jolly Jogger,
   Jolly Jogger, Jolly Jogger.
   Jog along with Jolly Jogger.
   Jolly Jogger.

Other Verses
For *jog*, substitute *jump*, *jitter*, *jiggle*, *jerk*.

38

ACTIONS

jog: run slowly in place

Other Actions
Do actions that the words for the other verses indicate.

ACTIVITIES

- If it's the season when pumpkins are plentiful, bring a jack-o'-lantern to class and carve it. The children can help by drawing parts of the face to be cut and scooping out the insides.

- Let the children make jewelry. Each child will need a needle and yarn or string and various kinds of things to string like styrofoam packing pieces, large macaroni, old beads, buttons, paper cut into interesting shapes, and other available materials.

- Have the children make jigsaw puzzles by cutting pictures from magazines into four or five big pieces. Have them put the pieces for each picture in an envelope and put the envelope on a table for others to use.

- Do a junk art project. Each child will need to bring from home paper, glue, and junk (old beads, leaves, buttons, and so on). Have the children arrange their junk on a piece of heavy paper and glue it down.

- Take the children on an imaginary journey to Japan. Bring in pictures, books, articles, and filmstrips showing Japanese life.

- Set aside a few minutes for a joke time. Let the children tell each other jokes they know. You could get them started with this one: "What falls down but doesn't get hurt?" (raindrops).

- Have the children recite "Jack Be Nimble" as they jump over a paper *J*.

- Open a jewelry center in your classroom. Ask the children to bring in different kinds of costume jewelry from home, and let them use it for dramatic play. If you can find several pairs of earrings, make a matching activity. Put all the earrings in a box. Let the children sort them into pairs.

- Find someone who knows how to juggle and ask him or her to perform for your class. Afterwards, let the children go outdoors to try juggling.

- Take the children outdoors for a few minutes of jogging each day.

- Let the children listen to some jazz music. While they listen, have them draw pictures of what the music makes them think of.

- Tell the children to locate the major joints in their bodies, feel them, and see how they move.

- Have the children play Jack-in-the-Box. Tell them to squat down as low as they can go and quietly say this poem:

Jack-in-the-box all shut up tight
Not a breath of air, not a peep of light.
Oh, how tired it must be!
Open the box and out jumps me.

ACTIONS

Jumps: clap hands and jump up

COOKING

Jiggling Jello

1 c. cold water   *2 pkg. unflavored gelatin*   *1/2 c. honey*
3 c. fruit juice (orange, grape, apple)   Optional: *fruit*

Sprinkle the gelatin into the water and place in a pan over medium heat, stirring constantly until dissolved. Add the remaining ingredients and stir well. Refrigerate the gelatin until it is set. When it is nearly set, add fruit, if desired, such as apple and banana chunks, canned pears, peaches, or fruit cocktail.

Kicky Kangaroo

Use Patterns 1 and 5.

STORY

My name is Kicky Kangaroo. I live in Kansas. The little bundle of fur in my pocket is my baby Kooky. Kooky and I kick around all day. We like to bring kites to kids in kindergarten. We live in an old kitchen no one ever uses. We keep our kernels and ketchup there. We carry keys so we don't get locked out of our kitchen.

SONG
(tune of "Row, Row, Row Your Boat")

1. Kick, kick, kick your feet,
   Kicky Kangaroo.
   Kickety, kickety, kickety, kickety,
   Kanga Ranga Roo.
2. Fly a kite, fly a kite,
   Kicky Kangaroo
   Kite, kite, kite, kite,
   Kanga Ranga Roo.

41

3. Pet a kitten, pet a kitten,
   Kicky Kangaroo.
   Kitten, kitten, kitten, kitten,
   Kanga Ranga Roo.
4. Turn your key, turn your key,
   Kicky Kangaroo.
   Key, key, key, key,
   Kanga Ranga Roo.
5. Eat a kernel, eat a kernel,
   Kicky Kangaroo.
   Kernel, kernel, kernel, kernel,
   Kanga Ranga Roo.

ACTIONS

kick: kick feet one at a time
kangaroo: jump up
kite: pretend to fly
kitten: pretend to pet one
key: turn an imaginary one
kernel: pretend to nibble

ACTIVITIES

- Teach the children to make a kite; each child will need paper, crayons, yarn, and scissors. Have the children find the approximate middle of each of the four sides of the paper and make a dot there. When the dots are connected by lines, a diamond shape for the body of the kite will appear. Have the children cut out the kites and glue or staple on a yarn tail. Let the children write the letter *K* on their kites.

- If weather permits, take the children outdoors and fly a kite sometime during *K* Week. You could make it a special event by letting the class find a package with a card in it from Kicky Kangaroo. The package could contain the kite.

- Bring a kaleidoscope to the classroom and let the children experiment with it. Then show the children how to make a kaleidoscope of their own. Each child will need a short length of cardboard tube, crayon shavings, wax paper, and a rubber band. First, place the shavings between two small pieces of wax paper and press the paper with an iron. When the paper has cooled, place it around one end of the tube and secure it with a rubber band. Hold the tube up to the light and move it around. Let the children exchange kaleidoscopes to see all the different patterns that were made.

- Have a karate expert demonstrate karate skills to the children.

- Have the children make kidney bean pictures. Let them glue the beans to construction paper to make pictures, designs, or *K*s, and add details with crayon.

- Let the class make a *kinder-garden* in which each child plants a flower he or she has made. The children will need large sheets of colorful paper, glue, scissors, and crayons. Have each child draw and cut out a large flower shape, which can be decorated with crayons or cut-out designs. Then have each child glue his or her own picture to the center of the flower. The portraits can be photos or pictures drawn by the children. All the flowers can be pinned to the bulletin board or glued to mural-size paper.

- Let the children practice kicking, coordinating their eye and feet movements. Let them kick beanbags, boxes, balls, and balloons.

- Tell a story about some kind act that Kicky could have done. Then let the children tell about something they once did or could do that shows kindness. The children could draw illustrations of kind acts, too.

- Have the children make kazoos. Each child will need a short length of cardboard tubing, a pencil, wax paper, and a rubber band. Tell the children to punch three holes in their tubes with the pencil. Then have them cover one end of the tube with wax paper, secured with a rubber band. The children can play the kazoos.

COOKING

Kabobs

pineapple chunks	*orange sections*	*marshmallows*	*apple chunks*
banana chunks	*pear chunks*	*raisins*	*carrot rounds* *toothpicks*

Have the children help cut up the various foods (or any other available fruits or vegetables) and place them in small dishes on tables. Let the children assemble their own kabobs on toothpicks, to suit their tastes.

Looney Lion

Use Patterns 1 and 11.

STORY

My name is Looney Lion. I live in a large lump. I like my lump a lot. I have lots of logs in my lump. I sleep on one, use one for a chair and one for a table, and I keep my treasures in another. I have lanterns in my lump to give me light. I live by a large lake, and sometimes when I go for walks, I get lost. When I'm not walking I like to play Little League Leap-Frog. We lions have the best leap-frog team in the land. We beat the leopards every time. Listen to me sing: "La, la, la, la!"

SONG
(tune of "People on the Bus")

1. Little Looney Lion lives in a lump,
   Lives in a lump, lives in a lump.
   Little Looney Lion lives in a lump.
   Lives in a lump, lump, lump.
2. Little Looney Lion likes lots of logs,
   Likes lots of logs, likes lots of logs.
   Little Looney Lion likes lots of logs.
   Lots of logs, logs, logs.

44

3. Little Looney Lion has lanterns in the lump,
   Lanterns in the lump, lanterns in the lump.
   Little Looney Lion has lanterns in the lump.
   Lanterns in the lump, lump, lump.
4. Looney Lion plays Little League Leap-Frog,
   Little League Leap-Frog, Little League Leap-Frog.
   Looney Lion plays Little League Leap-Frog.
   Little League Leap-Frog, Frog, Frog.

ACTIONS

lion: make ears with hands on head
lump: draw an imaginary lump in the air
logs: roll hands around each other
lanterns: pretend to carry one
leap-frog: jump

ACTIVITIES

• Set up a terrarium and put some lizards in it. Call the lizards Looney's Lovable Lizards. Let the children give the lizards *L* names.

• Have the children play I'm Thinking of Something, using *L* words. Some possible words are lace, lamb, lamp, lazy, leaf, lettuce, lollipop, love, litterbug, listen, lick, light, lemon, and lion.

• Teach the children a game called My Lap Is Laden. The first child begins with something like this: "My lap is laden with lemons." A second child could then say, "My lap is laden with lemons and lions." A third would repeat the sentence and add another *L* word, and so on around the room. This game is excellent for practicing listening skills and sequencing.

• Teach the children how to lace string or yarn. First, cut out a large *L* for each child and punch holes around the edges. (The children can do this, but the project will be much longer.) Give each child a length of string or yarn for lacing. Then show them how to bring the string through the holes: back to front, front to back, or in and out. This project is excellent for developing small-muscle coordination.

• Bring a lime and a lemon to school. Cut them into small pieces and give each child a sample of each fruit. Let the children compare the tastes. Then have them make a little chart and write something about each fruit. (The chart could be copied from one on the chalkboard or written by you on paper and traced over by the children.)

• Have the children cut lacelike decorations from small squares of lightweight paper in the same way they might cut paper snowflakes.

- Bring in and discuss with the class information about ladybugs. Then make a ladybug game out of oaktag. Cut out a number of ladybug shapes and decorate them by pairs. Have the children match the pairs by patterns or numbers of spots.

- Ask the children to make lions for Looney's Little League team. Each child will need brown and yellow paper, yarn for tails, cotton balls, and yellow chalk. Have the children cut out heads, necks, bodies, and four legs, and glue them together to make their lions. Then, let the children "dye" stretched-out cotton balls yellow by rubbing them in piles of yellow chalk dust on a paper towel. Have them glue the yellow balls around the lion's head, and glue one intact ball to the end of a yarn tail. When the tails are attached to the bodies, the lions can be decorated with Ls, leaves, or lace, if desired.

COOKING

Looney's Luscious Lemonade

1 lemon   water   honey   ice cubes

Provide the above ingredients for each group of two or three children. Have each pair or group of children roll their lemon on a table to soften it before squeezing. Then cut the lemon in half, and have the children squeeze the juice into paper cups. Let the children remove the seeds, and add water and a little honey to sweeten. Tell them to stir the lemonade well. Add ice cubes.

Looney's Likable Lollipops

1/2 lb. raisins (or half raisins and half dates)   1/2 lb. dried apricots
1 c. nuts   1 c. wheat germ   1/2 c. honey   lollipop sticks

Supply the above ingredients. Put fruits and nuts through a food grinder, if one is available, or have the children cut the fruit and nuts with small serrated plastic knives. Add to the rest of the ingredients. Let the children shape the mixture into balls and put the balls on sticks. One recipe makes four dozen small lollipops.

Merry Mouse

Use Patterns 1 and 4.

STORY

I am a little mouse named Merry. I live in a mushroom patch in Minneapolis, Minnesota. I am always munching on things that begin with the letter *M*. After a bit of munching, I say, "M-M-M-M." Sometimes I get into mischief because of all the munching I do. Once I munched the mail. Another time I munched on some magazines and mittens. I like to munch meat, mints, muffins, macaroni, malts, macaroons, mushrooms, and marshmallows.

SONG·
(tune of "Old MacDonald Had a Farm")

Merry Mouse loves to munch.
Munch, munch, munch, munch, munch.
Merry munches macaroni.
Munch, munch, munch, munch, munch.
With some macaroni here and some
    macaroni there;
Here some, there some, everywhere some macaroni.
Merry Mouse loves to munch.
Munch, munch, munch, munch, munch.

Other Verses

Substitute *meat, muffins, mushrooms,* and other *M* foods for *macaroni.* Sing as you would "Old MacDonald," and repeat previous foods after each new verse.

ACTIONS

munch: open and close hands in quick movements

ACTIVITIES

- Have each child cut out a large capital *M* from construction paper. (You may want to draw it for them.) Let the children make their *M*s into M-Monsters by drawing, coloring, and gluing strange or scary features on them.

- Open a center in your classroom for the use of magnets. Let the children handle the magnets and find out what they will and will not pick up. Have on hand paper clips, bobby pins, safety pins, plastic items, soft drink pop-tops, and so on.

- Let the children have the opportunity to talk about and handle some real money. You might wish to bring in coins from foreign countries.

- Have the children make a mural. Give the picture an *M* theme, perhaps monsters, creatures with mustaches, or mice.

- Show the class a movie about mountains, mice, men, or other *M* topics.

- Show the class how to make mittens. Each child will need paper, scissors, and yarn. Have the children work in pairs, tracing around each other's hands in the shape of a mitten. Have them cut out the mittens, poke a hole in each one, draw the yarn through the hole, and hang them from a clothesline.

- Bring a microscope or magnifying glass to class. Let the children see various objects magnified through the glass.

- Have a mail carrier visit the classroom and tell about his or her job.

- Make up a class story about the mystery of the missing moose (mosquito, mule, monster). Let each child tell part of the story and illustrate a favorite part when the story is done.

- Have the class play I'm Thinking of Something, using *M* words. Some possible words are milk, moon, mail, money, mirror, magic, monkey, moose, mustache, and melt.

- Tell the children all about maps and what they depict. Then let the children make a map of the classroom.

• Talk about the moon, and show pictures of what it looks like. Then have the children take an imaginary trip there with you. Pretend when you get there that you run into a moon monster. Let the children tell you what it looks like to them. They can draw or paint it if they wish.

COOKING

Merry's Marvelous Malts

about 3 quarts ice cream (preferably without preservatives)
enough milk to make malts of the correct consistency

Mix the malts in a giant bowl with an electric mixer, or let each child or small group of children shake the malts themselves in a jar.

M-M-M-Good Meatballs

1 lb. hamburger   1/2 c. dry bread crumbs   1/2 c. evaporated milk
1 egg   1 t. salt   1/4 t. pepper
Optional: *1 grated raw apple*

Mix all the ingredients together, and form them into balls. Brown the meatballs on all sides in a lightly greased electric skillet. Serve.

Noisy Newt

Use Pattern 1.

STORY

My name is Noisy Newt. I live in a nice new nest in northern Nevada. I am very noisy—all day long I make a noise like this: "N-N-N-N-N!" At night, I like to pound nails. Sometimes I am a nuisance with all my noise. So, I take a nap at noon. At least it is quiet then. When I'm not napping or making noise I like to look at people's noses. I don't have one, so I just look at others and imagine what I'd look like with one. My favorite foods to nibble on are noodles and nuts. My favorite number is nine. I like to sing "9" nine times, like this: "9-9-9-9-9-9-9-9-9." My noodle necklace has nine noodles.

SONG
(tune of "Jimmy Crack Corn")

Noisy goes nodding, nod, nod, nod.
Noisy goes nodding, nod, nod, nod.
Noisy goes nodding, nod, nod, nod.
Nod for Noisy Newt.
Other Verses
Substitute *napping, nesting, nibbling,* and *nailing* for *nod.*

50

ACTIONS

nod: drop head in short, jerky movements

Other Actions
napping: turn head to side and rest
nesting: squat down
nibbling: open and close hands quickly
nailing: make hammering motions

ACTIVITIES

- Have the class make noodle necklaces. Give each child nine large rigatoni noodles and a length of yarn for stringing.

- Have the children go on a newspaper hunt for *N*s. Tell the children to cut out all the capital and small *N*s they can find (let each child look on one page) and glue them down to plain sheets of paper. When they have finished, let each child count his or her *N*s and write the number on the paper.

- Have the children make nail-nose faces. Each child will need a small square of wood, a nail for a nose, markers for drawing the rest of the face, glue, and yarn for the hair. Have several hammers available for the children to pound in their nail-noses.

- Show the children how to make Nifty Nosegay flowers out of napkins. Each child will need several paper napkins, a pipe cleaner, and a dab of perfume. Have the children cut a circle from the napkins, put all the circles together, and find the middle. Then have the children pinch the middle together and wrap the end of a pipe cleaner around it, making the stem. Let the children put a drop of perfume on their nosegays so their noses can smell them.

- Hold a classroom Nifty Noise Contest. Tell the children about the contest ahead of time so they can put together a noisemaker. On the specified day, tell everyone to bring in their noisemakers, and hold a contest. Let the children vote for the noisemaker that makes the niftiest noise.

- Let the children make play-dough nests. Before they begin, add yellow food coloring to part of the dough for the nests and blue to some of the play-dough for eggs. Give each child a ball of each color and have the children form nests and then egg shapes to set in them. Let the nests and eggs dry for several days. The children can then cut out paper birds and set them in the nests.

- Paint noses. Let children look in a mirror to paint their own noses. Use a light color paint (white or yellow) to make cleanup easier. Children can work in pairs to paint each other's noses.

Play-dough

2 c. flour   *1 T. oil*   *1 c. salt*   *1 c. water*

Mix the ingredients into a dough. Knead with your hands.

- Encourage the children to put together a class newspaper. Let every child have a chance to contribute part of it. The newspaper could contain songs, stories, news, and jokes, as well as pictures.
- Talk about nicknames. Let everyone pick out a nickname to be called during *N* Week.
- Invite a nurse to come and speak to the children about his or her profession.
- Have the children work with the number 9. Teach them to write it, and ask them to draw pictures with nine objects in each.
- Tell the children some facts about newts. Let the class draw pictures of newts and give the newts *N* names.

COOKING

Noisy's Nutty Nuts

3 c. nuts   *3 T. butter*   *1 t. dry mustard*   *1 t. chili powder*
1-1/2 t. salt

Melt the butter over low heat and add the nuts. Stir the mixture until brown (about 5 minutes). Remove from heat and drain. Stir in the spices, then cool. Nibble!

Polka Pig

Use Pattern 1.

STORY

My name is Polka Pig. I carry a pompom and a pine cone wherever I go.
I also wear a pumpkin patch, a peace sign, petunias, and pearls. I can
play the piano perfectly. I live on a porch near a pool in Pittsburgh,
Pennsylvania. I love to eat, like most pigs, but I eat only foods that begin
with *P*, like popcorn, pizza, pancakes, potatoes, pumpkin pie, pumpkin
seeds, pineapple, pickles, and pretzels.

SONG
(tune of "Are You Sleeping?")

1. Are you playing? Are you playing?
    Polka Pig? Polka Pig?
    Playing your piano. Playing your piano.
    Ping, pong, ping. Ping, pong, ping.
2. Are you peeling? Are you peeling?
    Polka Pig? Polka Pig?
    Peeling your potatoes. Put them in your pockets.
    Peel, Polka, peel. Peel, Polka, peel.

3. Are you eating? Are you eating?
   Polka Pig? Polka Pig?
   Pineapple and pizza, potatoes and popcorn.
   Pop, pop, pop. Pop, pop, pop.

ACTIONS

playing: pretend to play the piano
peeling: pretend to peel potatoes
eating: pretend to eat

ACTIVITIES

- Have the class make pink paper *P*s. Then pin a large pink pocket on the bulletin board, and let the children put their pink *P*s in Polka's Pink Pocket.

- Have the children paint large pink-and-purple polka dots on pigs drawn on light pink paper.

- Bring a parachute into the classroom, and let the children experiment with it. Position the children around it evenly, and let them move it up and down, run in circles around it, get under it, and so on.

- Hold a Push the P Relay. Divide the class into two teams and tell the children they must *push* (not kick) *P* with their foot to a designated line and back. Each child must say the letter name before passing the letter to the next member of the team.

- Have the children paint purple people pictures. Let the class show in their drawings what the world would be like if people were purple.

- Teach the children a simple polka step. Play some hearty polka music, and let the class have fun moving to the music.

- Make a very large pumpkin, full of holes so it looks worn out. Attach it to a wall or bulletin board in your classroom. Tell the children the pumpkin got worn out from being carried around so much, as it is a particularly pleasing pumpkin. Ask them to help patch the pumpkin, using squares of paper and paste.

- Have a Planting Party. Each child will need a small milk carton or paper cup filled with soil. Let the children plant petunia seeds in their cartons.

- Have a People Parade. Tell the children ahead of time to wear something pink, purple, polka-dotted or plaid on the chosen day. Play some music and have the children parade around the room.

- Open a puzzle center in your room. Put all the puzzles you can find in one area for the children to use during *P* Week.

- If the school is near a suitable area, take the children there to collect pine cones. Then let the children make a pine cone pyramid by gluing the pine cones together. They could also glue pine cones to cardboard to make pine cone pictures.

COOKING

Popcorn

popcorn   oil   salt

Pop the corn in oil in a popper or large pot according to directions. While the popcorn cooks, let the children say the popcorn poem, acting out what the words say as they recite the poem. Tell them to jump on the word *popcorn*. Salt the corn, and eat it.

Pop, pop, pop! Pour the corn in the pot.
Pop, pop, pop! Shake it till it's hot.
Pop, pop, pop! Lift the lid. What have you got?
Pop, pop, pop—popcorn!

Pumpkin Seeds

pumpkin seeds   salt   butter

Wash and dry the seeds from the inside of a pumpkin. Fry the seeds in butter in an electric skillet until browned (about 15 minutes). Salt the seeds lightly, and enjoy them.

Quacky Quacker

Use Pattern 1.

STORY

My name is Quacky Quacker. I love to quack, especially when it is very quiet—then everyone can hear me. Some people think I have a queer quack. But I like my quack. My job is making quilts. I work very quickly and quietly except for an occasional quack. I never quit until I have finished a quilt. Sometimes I like to quiver and quake all over. After a good swim, I quiver a lot until I am dry. If other quackers make fun of me, I quarrel with them. But I don't like to quarrel, so I try to quit quarreling quickly.

SONG
(tune of "Hail, Hail, the Gang's All Here")

Quack! Quack! Our quacker is here.
Quacky is our quacker,
A very quick quacker.
Quack! Quack! Our quacker is here.
Quick quack now for Quacky.
Other Verses
Substitute these words for the word *quack* in the last line: *quit, quiet, quiver, quarrel.*

ACTIONS

quack: put hands together near mouth to form duck beak
quick: pretend to hurry

Other Actions
Do actions that the words for the other verses indicate.

ACTIVITIES

- Have the children do "quick" activities. Call out the following directions one right after the other: walk, run, skip, raise hands, tap feet, bend over, blink eyes, and turn around.
- Invite the children to make a classroom quilt. Let each child decorate a five-inch square of paper with *Q*s or pictures of things that begin with *Q*. A quilt could also be made from fabric pieces decorated with felt-tip marking pens (use permanent ink if the quilt is to be washed) and sewn together. The finished quilt can be hung on a wall.
- Invite a skilled quilter to talk to the children about quiltmaking.
- Discuss with the children what a quarterback is. Have the children paint pictures of quarterbacks with *Q*s on their shirts.
- Let the children examine quarters (give one to every two or three children). Then take the children to a store to see what a quarter will buy.
- Ask the children to make some friends for Quacky Quacker out of modeling clay. They may also wish to roll capital and small *Q*s out of clay.
- Take the class to the library to find out about quails. When they return to the classroom, ask the children to draw pictures of quails.
- Give the children a Quarters Quiz. Tell each child to fold a sheet of paper in quarters. Give them something to do in each quarter; for example, draw a red circle, make an 8, draw a house, draw a polka-dot box, draw horizontal lines, make an *X*, draw your face, write your name. Correct their work when the quiz is completed.

COOKING

Quick Quack Bread (requires oven)

3 mashed bananas	*1-1/2 c. sugar or honey*	*4-1/2 T. milk*	*3 eggs*
3/4 c. melted butter	*1/3 t. salt*	*1 t. vanilla*	*3 c. flour*
1 t. soda	*1 t. baking powder*	Optional: *1/2 c. chopped nuts*	

Mix all the above ingredients and bake in loaf pans at 350° F. for about 45 minutes. One recipe makes two large loaves.

Quicky Quacks

8 c. apple juice　　　*2 c. applesauce*　　　*ice cream sticks*

Mix the ingredients well. Put the mixture into ice cube trays or small paper cups, and freeze it until nearly firm. Add ice cream sticks. Continue freezing until firm. Eat the *snack-on-a-stick*. (The juice and sauce mixture may also be put in paper cups, frozen until nearly firm, and eaten with a spoon as a slushy treat.)

Racing Raccoon

Use Patterns 1 and 9.

STORY

My name is Racing Raccoon. I am a red raccoon who is always racing around. Sometimes I race on a raft on the river. I have rosy cheeks and rick-rack on my shirts. I wear a ring on a red ribbon around my neck. I am a rascal sometimes because I like to roar and scare the roosters on my ranch. I like to read recipes and eat raisins, radishes, roasts, and rabbits. When I am not racing my raft I listen to rock-and-roll records. I love to rock and roll in my room.

SONG
(tune of "Row, Row, Row Your Boat")

Row, row, row, your raft,
Racing Raccoon.
Rickety rackety rickety rackety
Round and round and round.

ACTIONS

row: pretend to row
raccoon: make circles with fingers around eyes

rickety rackety: move fingers up and down
round: swing arms in large circles

ACTIVITIES

- Take the children outdoors to collect rocks. Then let the children make paperweights by painting their rocks and spraying them with shellac.

- Have a variety of relay races. Let the children race by running or rolling like logs.

- Play a game with the children called Bounce-a-Rhyme. Choose a child to start the game and give him or her a ball. Then tell the child a word to try to rhyme. Each time a rhyming word is thought of, the child should say the word and bounce the ball. For example, if the beginning word is *cat*, a bounce could be made for *rat, hat, sat, mat,* and so on. When the child can think of no more rhyming words, the ball should be passed to the right and that child can be given a new word to rhyme.

- Have a Roaring Contest. Do this outdoors so you will not have to worry about disturbing other classes.

- Play a listening game for *R* words. Tell the children that when they hear an *R* word they should move like a robot. Be sure to intersperse other words with those that start with the letter *R*.

- Do an experiment on rusting. Put water in several metal containers (jar lids work well). Then leave nails, paper clips, bobby pins, bottle caps, plastic items, and whatever else the children may suggest in the water for several days. Check the results. Discuss.

- Have the children draw a capital and small *R* on a sheet of paper, and glue rice grains on the lines.

- Let the children play a game called Red Rover. Divide the class into two equal teams and have the teams stand at opposite goals, holding hands in a line. Tell one team to call out to the other, "Red Rover, Red Rover, send someone (Suzie, Bill, or someone else) right over!" The person named must run to the opposite line and try to break through between two children. If the child does not succeed in breaking through, he or she becomes a member of the new team. If the child does break through, one of the children whose hands were broken through is chosen by the runner to be added to the runner's team.

- Bring in several pictures or books (or both) about rhinoceroses. Discuss them with the class.

- Let the children tell their favorite riddles. A book of riddles might get things started.

- Show the children how roots grow by putting a sweet potato in a glass of water and watching the results.

- Have the children listen to some rock-and-roll music. Ask the class why they think the music got that name. Let the children move to the music.
- Introduce the class to the rectangle. Ask the children to find rectangular objects in the room. Then let the children assemble a rectangle picture by cutting out many different sizes and colors of paper rectangles and pasting them on a large piece of paper.

COOKING

Racing's Recipe for Ridiculous Rabbits

1 piece of lettuce   1 pear half (drain well if you use canned)
2 raisins   2 blanched toasted almonds
1 piece of unsweetened coconut   1 spoonful of yogurt or cottage cheese

Provide the above ingredients for each child, then let each child assemble a Ridiculous Rabbit, using the lettuce for bedding, the pear half for the body, the raisins for eyes, the almonds for ears, the coconut for the mouth, and the yogurt for the tail.

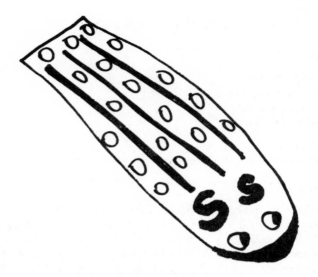

Spotty Snake

Use Pattern 3.

STORY

My name is Spotty Snake. I love spots. I have them all over my body. I have some stripes, too. I live under the stairs at Sunshine School. I love to slip and slide around on my snake skin. Sometimes I slide around with a spider or a salamander, but most of the time I slide with other snakes. I surprise everyone with a sound like this: "S-S-S-S-S-!" I eat sandwiches, sauerkraut, salad, and sausages. My favorite numbers are six and seven. I am a special snake who loves to sing solos and hear others singing. Sometimes I am silly.

SONG
(tune of "Down by the Station")

Down by the school slipping in the sand
I see a special snake
Spotty is its name.
See the silly Spotty?
Striped and spotted Spotty.
S-S-S-S (sound)
Spotty Snake.
Other Verses
Substitute *swimming, skating,* and *sleeping* for *slipping.*

ACTIONS

slipping: slip with feet
snake: make glasses with hands around eyes
S-S: stretch high on first two *S*s
S-S: bend low on last two *S*s

Other Actions
Do appropriate actions for the words in the other verses.

ACTIVITIES

- Have the class make Silly Sacks. Each child will need a lunch sack, newspaper, yarn for a tie, yarn for hair, and crayons or felt-tip marking pens. Tell the children to stuff their sacks with the newspaper and tie the opening with yarn. Then let them decorate their sacks to make them look silly. The children can also work in groups to put on Silly Sack puppet shows. Lunch sacks could be made into Sad Sacks as well.

- Have a classroom demonstration on steam. Put some water in a pan. Place the pan on a hot plate. When the water boils, discuss what has happened and the uses to which steam can be put.

- Take the children to a store, and let them point out all the things that begin with *S* (strawberries, sweet potatoes, sauce, sunflower seeds, and so on).

- Have the children do exercises that begin with *S*: sit-ups, skipping, sliding, stretching, and swaying.

- Hold a sing-along with another class or two. Have Spotty visible. Let your children tell the visitors who Spotty is and why they are singing (because Spotty loves singing).

- Have the children gather some old socks and make friends for Spotty. Let them stuff the socks with paper and glue on eyes, mouths, and spots made of colored paper, pieces of material, or buttons.

- Have the children make straw pictures. Each child will need several straws, paper, scissors, glue, and crayons. Tell the children to cut their straws into various lengths and glue them down on paper to make a picture or design. The straws could also be formed into *S*s.

- Take the children to a slide in a nearby park or playground and have a special sliding party. Let each child have six or seven slides for Spotty. Bring Spotty along.

- Take the class on an imaginary safari. Ask the children to think of all the *S* animals they can hunt for (snakes, seals, salamanders, squirrels, sea horses, sunfish, and skunks).

COOKING

Silly Sandwiches

bread   a variety of the following: *ketchup, raisins, peanut butter, cream cheese, yogurt, jelly, pickles, bananas, mustard, chocolate chips, wheat germ, honey, butter, applesauce, hulled sunflower seeds, coconut*

Provide one or two slices of bread for each child. Let the children make Silly Sandwiches by spreading unusual food combinations on their bread.

Tricky Turkey

Use Pattern 2.

STORY

My name is Tricky Turkey. I'm called that because I can do tricks that no
other turkey can do, like playing a tambourine with my toes, talking on
a telephone, and tossing tangerines. I am also good at tumbling. I wear a
tutu that has a tie for tumbling. I have two teeth and a tongue and two
toes on each foot. My favorite flowers are tulips, and my favorite
numbers are two and ten. I live in a tan tent in Texas. My best friends are
a tiger and a turtle. We play Tag together in a tunnel.

SONG
(tune of "If You're Happy and You Know It")

Tricky Turkey says right now to touch your toes.
Tricky Turkey says right now to touch your toes.
Touch your toes, touch your toes, touch your toes,
    touch your toes.
Tricky Turkey says right now to touch your toes.
Other Verses
Substitute the following for *touch your toes: trace a* T, *twirl around, do the
twist, touch two teeth, touch your tongue, drive a truck.*

ACTIONS

toes: reach down and touch toes

Other Actions
Do appropriate actions for the words in the other verses.

ACTIVITIES

- Have the children draw a tiny television set on a tiny sheet of paper, and then draw a picture of something that begins with a *T* on the tiny screen.
- Bring in several toy phones, and talk about how to use the telephone. Discuss good telephone manners.
- Let the children crawl through a canvas tunnel during *T* Week.
- Teach the class how to play Tunnel Ball. Tell the children to form a circle with their legs spread apart, foot-to-foot with the child on either side. Choose one child to be It. Have It stand in the center of the circle with a ball. Tell It to try to throw the ball through someone's *tunnel* (between their legs), while the children try to stop the ball with their hands. If the ball goes through someone's tunnel, that child becomes It. After the children are more skilled at this game, several children at once can be Its. This variation is more difficult but lots of fun.
- Have the class make towers or totem poles from grocery boxes. Let the children paint the towers and decorate them with *T*s.
- Bring a tape recorder into the classroom. Record the children singing Tricky Turkey's song.
- At recess or gym time, let the children play Tag. Chalk a giant T on the playground for the *safe* area.
- Bring in some objects and materials with some interesting textures and let the class have a Touching Time.
- Let the children make a giant train. Each child can make a car for the train using grocery boxes, paper, paint, crayons, scissors, and glue.
- Let each child make a small tablet by stapling several sheets of paper together. Have the children practice making *T*s on their tablets and draw pictures of objects that begin with the letter *T*.
- Make Tuesday a special day during *T* Week. Let the children make paper tulips to wear, and encourage the class to wear tennis shoes. Have toast for snack time.

COOKING

Tricky's Terrific Tacos

1 lb. hamburger   taco shells   1-1/2 c. shredded cheese
2 c. shredded lettuce   1-1/2 c. chopped tomatoes

Let the children help prepare the cheese, lettuce, and tomatoes and put these in small bowls on tables. Brown the hamburger. Put a small bowl of it on each table. Let each child fill a taco shell with meat and any of the other ingredients. If you would like to make your own taco shells, follow the recipe below.

Tricky's Terrific Taco Shells

1-1/2 c. flour   1-1/2 c. corn meal   2 c. cold water   2 eggs
cooking oil or shortening

Mix the flour and corn meal. Add the water and egg. Beat the mixture until it is smooth. If necessary, add a little more water to make the batter the consistency of whipping cream. In a skillet, melt about 1 t. of the shortening over medium-high heat. Pour about 1/4 c. of the batter into the skillet, tilting the skillet to coat the bottom. Cook the shell until dry on top (about one minute). Turn the shell over and cook the other side. After frying, cover the shells so they don't dry out. Taco shells can be made ahead of time and frozen.

Vam Vampire

Use Patterns 1 and 11.

STORY

My name is Vam. I am a vampire! I wear a veil with a pretty violet on it in front of my very scary face. My teeth are *V* fangs. My nose is shaped like a *V*. I always wear a vest. I have lots of vim, vigor, and vitality because I eat plenty of vegetables and take my vitamins. Most vampires drink blood, but not me! I drink vinegar! Vinegar is so velicious! My favorite thing to do is stand and vibrate.

SONG
(tune of "Farmer in the Dell")

1. Vam is a vampire. Oh, Vam is a vampire.
   V-V-V-V-V-V-V, Vam is a vampire.
2. Vam drinks vinegar. Oh, Vam drinks vinegar.
   V-V-V-V-V-V-V, Vam drinks vinegar.
3. Vam eats vegetables. Oh, Vam eats vegetables.
   V-V-V-V-V-V-V, Vam eats vegetables.
4. Vam wears a veil. Oh, Vam wears a veil.
   V-V-V-V-V-V-V, Vam wears a veil.
5. Vam likes to vibrate. Oh, Vam likes to vibrate.
   V-V-V-V-V-V-V, Vam likes to vibrate.

ACTIONS

V: make *V* with fingers
drinks: pretend to drink from a cup
eats: pretend to eat
veil: cover face with hands
vibrate: shake body all over

ACTIVITIES

- Have a vegetable-tasting party. With the children's help, cut up a variety of vegetables into bite-sized pieces for tasting.
- Give each child a drop of vinegar to taste. Talk about the different foods vinegar is used in (to make pickles, in dressing, and so on).
- Let the children make valentines for Vam. Show the class how to cut a heart shape, and let them decorate the valentines as they wish.
- Let the children play Hide-and-Seek outdoors, but call the game Vanish.
- Have a voting day. First, decide on a topic or thing to vote for. Then, let the children register, vote, count the votes, and talk about the process when it is all over.
- Let each child cut a shape out of a small piece of velvet, glue it to a sheet of paper, and make a picture around it. Talk about velvet's unusual texture.
- Plan an imaginary vacation with your class. Then pretend to go on it.
- Have the children make vases using empty juice cans. Let them decorate the vases as they wish.
- Pour some vinegar into a glass jar, add some baking soda, and listen—you should hear the sound of the letter *V*!
- Bring a bunch of violets or an African violet plant to school for *V* Week. The children can draw violets or make their own violets from paper.
- Ask a veterinarian to come and speak to the children about his or her job.
- Show the children how to make vests. Each child will need scissors, a large grocery sack, and crayons. Tell the children to cut the front of the sack down the middle (making sure to cut all the way) to make the front

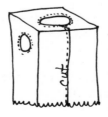

opening of the vest. Then have them cut a hole for the head in the bottom of the sack and an armhole on either side. The children may decorate the sack any way they desire. Encourage the children to write *V*s somewhere on their vests.

COOKING

Vanilla Vudding

1 c. sugar   3/4 c. cornstarch   1/2 t. salt   8-1/4 c. milk
6 T. butter   3 t. vanilla extract

Mix together the sugar, cornstarch, and salt. Gradually stir in the milk until smooth. Cook the mixture over medium heat until it comes to a boil; let it boil for one minute. Remove the pudding from heat. Stir in the butter and vanilla. Pour the pudding into small cups, and let it cool.

Vanishing Vegetable Soup

large soup bone   water   seasonings
variety of vegetables (carrots, celery, peas, corn, potatoes, beans, tomatoes, onions, or others)

This project will take two days unless you use a prepared beef or chicken broth instead of making one. On the first day, put the soup bone in water in a big pan with a lid. Cook the broth slowly for several hours, and refrigerate it overnight. On the second day remove the soup bone and put the broth back on the stove. Add to the broth cut-up vegetables that the children have prepared. Cook the soup until the vegetables are tender. Serve the soup in small cups or bowls—and watch it vanish!

Wacky Walrus

Use Pattern 1.

STORY

My name is Wacky Walrus. I am a wooly, wooly walrus with whiskers and a wig. I live in a white wigwam in the wilderness. With me lives my little friend Wiggly Worm. Wiggly and I waddle around whistling and whispering. When we are not waddling, we like to waltz around singing "Wah, wah, wah, wah!"

SONG
(tune of "Doggie in the Window")

How much is that walrus in the window—
The one with the wiggly worm?
How much is that walrus in the window?
Let's wink now for Wacky Walrus. Wink, wink!
Other Verses
Substitute *wiggle*, *waddle*, *waltz*, and *weep* for *wink*.

ACTIONS

walrus: make tusks with fingers
wiggly: wiggle like a worm

71

window: form a square with fingers
wink: wink

Other Actions
Do appropriate actions for words in other verses.

ACTIVITIES

- Have a waddling race. After dividing the class into teams, let the teams give themselves *W* names such as the Worms, the Walruses, and so on. After each child has waddled to a goal line and back, he or she must say "W" to the next waddler.

- Let the children make wishing windows. Give each child a sheet of white paper. Tell the children to fold the paper in half. Have the children cut three windows in the top half of the page (by drawing three squares with space in between and cutting them out). Under each window, tell the children to draw one wish they hope will come true. The children can share their wishes with the class or take them home to show their parents.

- Make a wigwam from an old sheet and broomsticks or poles during *W* Week.

- Teach the children how to weave. First, cut out a number of paper strips, or let the children do it. Then demonstrate how the strips can be woven in and out and glued down at the ends to a piece of construction paper. Remind the children as they work to alternate the strip patterns; that is, if they begin by going *over* on the first strip, they must begin by going *under* on the next. Ask the children to weave placemats for snack time.

- Share pictures of and information about woodpeckers with the children. Then let the children draw their own woodpecker pictures.

- Whip cream. Let the children eat it on slices of fruit for snack time.

- Let the children make wacky paper witches. Each child will need three black triangles—one for a hat and two for the body—glue, colored paper, crayons, and scissors. Have the children glue the triangles to the paper, and add witchlike features with crayons.

- Let the class have a Whispering Time. For a certain amount of time (set a timer), everyone must whisper instead of talking out loud.

- Have the class play a listening game with *W* words. Whenever the children hear a *W* word, tell them they should wink. Remember to intersperse other words with the words that begin with the letter *W*.

- Proclaim Wednesday of *W* Week official *W* Day, and have the children do a variety of projects: make witch hats with *W*s on them to wear, make paper worms like Wiggly to carry around, decorate the classroom windows with paper *W*s, welcome in a special way everyone who comes to visit that day.

- Teach the children this poem about wiggling:

  I wiggle my fingers, I wiggle my toes,
  I wiggle my shoulders, I wiggle my nose.
  Now, no more wiggles are left in me,
  And I am as still as still can be.

COOKING

Wagons

3- to 4-inch piece of celery   *four carrot rounds (slices)*
peanut butter   *toothpicks*

Provide the above ingredients for each child. Then have the children assemble their wagons by inserting two toothpicks through the celery at the top and the bottom, attaching the carrot rounds to the toothpicks, and loading the wagon with peanut butter.

X-Ray X

Use Patterns 1 and 9.

STORY

My name is X-Ray X. I live in the land of X-X-X. Everything there is in the shape of an X. One day, as I was carrying some of my X rays to a meeting, I heard a lot of shouting. I looked in the room where it was coming from, where men and women were talking loudly about something called an alphabet. I like to give extra help, and I give excellent advice. So I walked in and told them who I was and asked if I could help. They said they were naming letters and had named them all except for the one that looked like two crossed diagonal lines. The people had tried all kinds of names for this letter, such as *zoot*, *filit*, *schlam*, and *blump*, but none seemed quite right. Then one of the people asked if the letter could be named after me—X—and everyone thought that was a good idea. I told them it was fine with me. All the people were happy to have solved their alphabet problem, and I was glad to have helped them. I was excited because they had named a letter after me.

SONG
(tune of "One Little, Two, Three Little Indians")

1. *X-Ray X sings:*	I am X-Ray X-X-X.
	From the land of X-X-X.
	X-Ray X is my name.
	X rays are my greatest fame.
2. *People:*	May we use you, Dr. X,
	In our famous alphabet?
	We have all the letters but one.
	May we use your X for fun?
3. *X-Ray X:*	I am X-Ray X-X-X,
	From the land of X-X-X.
	You can use my X for fun.
	In your alphabet, I'm done.

4. A-B-C-D-E-F-G
H-I-J-K-L-M-N-O-P
Q-R-S and T-U-V
W-X-Y and Z.

ACTIONS
land of X-X-X: make *X*s with fingers
X: clap

ACTIVITIES

- Have the children act out the story of X-Ray X as a musical or a play. All the children except the one who portrays X-Ray X will be cast as participants in the alphabet meeting.

- Teach the children to play tick-tack-toe. Later you can hold a tick-tack-toe tournament.

- Have the class draw pictures of what they think X-Ray X's house looks like.

- Ask the children to make collages of *X*s. Each child can cut out construction paper *X*s or *X*s from a newspaper. The children can glue the letters on paper in interesting designs.

- Have the class do jumping jack exercises. Tell the children to stop when their bodies are in the shape of an *X* and to call out "X" at that point.

- Tell the children to use their imaginations to make *X* People. Give each child two ice cream sticks and glue. Have a supply of old beads, buttons, trim, and so on, on hand. Have the children glue down their sticks in the shape of an *X* and add details by gluing on other items. Crayons can also be used to add color and interest.

- Divide the class into teams and have an *X* Relay. Each team will need two sticks, placed on the floor about eight feet from the starting point. Have the first child on each team run to the sticks, make an *X* out of them, and run back to tag the next runner. The next runner should run to the sticks, take the *X* apart, and so on.

- Ask your doctor's office for any old X rays that are not needed and bring them to the class for the children to look at. Dentists' offices may have old X rays, too, but they will be small.

- Let the children roll *X*s out of modeling clay.

COOKING

X-Ray X's Xs

2 c. whole wheat flour   2 c. white flour   1 t. salt
3 T. oil   water   butter   Optional: honey, jelly

Mix together all the ingredients except the butter. Knead the dough for 5 to 10 minutes. (Use enough water to make a soft dough and add more flour if the dough becomes sticky.) Divide the dough into balls so the children can help. Put all the dough back into a bowl, cover with a damp cloth, and let it rest up to 45 minutes or an hour. Then shape the dough into balls the size of large marbles. Give each child two dough balls, and have the children form *X*s with them. When the *X*s are made, pat them flat and fry them in butter over medium heat. Fry a few *X*s at a time, adding more butter as needed. Serve the *X* crackers with butter and honey or jelly.

Yodeling Yak

Use Patterns 1 and 11.

STORY

My name is Yodeling Yak. I love the color yellow. I am almost
completely yellow myself. I have a yellow body, long yellow fur, and
yellow horns. I love to yodel. Listen to me: "Yo-da-lay-he-who!
Yo-da-lay-he-who!" I also like to yell and yank ropes with my mouth. I
will never say "no" to anyone. If you ask me a question, I'll always
answer "yes." I live on a yellow yacht. I eat yams, yeast bread, and
yummy yogurt.

SONG
(tune of "Are You Sleeping?")

Yodeling Yak,
Yodeling Yak,
Likes yellow,
Likes yellow.
Yahoo for Yodeling Yak,
Yahoo for Yodeling Yak,
Yo-da-lay-he-who, yo-da-lay-he-who.
Other Verses
For *yellow* substitute Ys, *yoyos, to yell and yank.*

77

ACTIONS

yak: make horns on head
yellow: pretend to color
yahoo: shake arm as though you are cheering
yo-da-lay-he-who: cup hands around mouth

Other Actions
Do appropriate actions for the words in the other verses.

ACTIVITIES

- Have the children make yellow yarn pictures. Each child will need yellow paper, a long piece of yellow yarn, glue, and scissors. Ask the children to glue pieces of yarn to the paper to make an interesting picture or design. The children could also make yellow yarn *Y*s.

- Have several children bring yoyos to school and let everyone have a chance to manipulate them. If you know someone who is an expert at yoyoing, ask that person to perform for the class.

- Discuss yoga with the children, or have an experienced person come in and demonstrate if you cannot. Then let the children try some simple exercises.

- Let the children make yarn drop pictures. Each child will need one piece of yarn 12 to 15 inches long, a cup of glue, and a piece of wax paper. Have the children dip pieces of yarn into the glue and drop it on the wax paper in a design. The children can sprinkle the design with glitter if it's available. Hang the yarn drops from string when they are dry.

- Have a tug-of-war but call it a Yanking Contest. Let the children compete on a one-to-one basis or in groups.

- Teach the children the song "Yankee Doodle." Then show the class how to make paper Yankee Doodle hats, and let the children wear the hats while they march around the room and sing.

fold in half

fold corners down

fold bottoms up

- Have a Yard Cleaning Day. Provide a number of sacks for collecting trash around the schoolyard. Remind the children to be very careful about picking up glass and other things with sharp edges.

- Let the children go outdoors and yell! You could even have a yelling contest to see who can yell the loudest.

- Share some pictures and information with the children about yaks. Have the children draw or paint pictures of yaks and write the word *yak* on their pictures.

- Discuss the meaning and makeup of a year. Bring in several types of calendars to show the children. Write the number of the year on the chalkboard. Let the children copy it.

COOKING

Yummy Yogurt

plain yogurt   powdered milk   slices of different fruits

Children decide what fruits to make Yummy Yogurt with. You can have a large variety, a couple, or one. Bananas, pears, peaches, blueberries, strawberries, and apricots all work well. Give each child about two spoonsful of fruit to put in a bowl and mash (have them use a fork or spoon for mashing). Ad 1 t. of powdered milk and about 1/4 c. yogurt to each bowl, and tell the children to mix well and enjoy. Yummy!

Zippy Zebra

Use Patterns 1 and 11.

STORY

My name is Zippy Zebra. I live in a very zany zoo. I like to zoom around.
Have you ever seen a zebra zoom? I have a real zipper on my body that
zips up and down. I love to zip and unzip it. All the animals in my zoo
have zip codes on their cages. I love the number zero. My zip code is
00000. Whenever I go out for a walk, I move in a zigzag pattern, never in
a straight line. My favorite food is zucchini.

SONG
(tune of "Did You Ever See a Lassie?")

1. Did you ever see a zebra, a zebra, a zebra?
   Did you ever see a zebra in a zany, zany zoo?
   Did you ever see a zebra, a zebra, a zebra?
   Did you ever see a zebra go zip, zip, zip, zip?

Other Verses

Substitute: *zoom*, *zigzag*, and *zero* for *zip*. On the last verse sing the entire
tune saying "Z."

80

ACTIONS

zebra: put outstretched fingers across face like stripes
zany: act silly
zip: pretend to zip a zipper

Other Actions
Do appropriate actions for the words in the other verses.

ACTIVITIES

- Have the children pretend to be zinnia seeds. Each time you call out a Z word, the children should grow a little (have them start in a squatting position and slowly stand up). Remember to intersperse other words with Z words.

- Have the class create a Zany Zoo, letting each child make silly animals for it. Encourage the children to think of different ways to make their animals zany, using paper, scissors, glue, beads, buttons, material scraps, trims, cotton balls, and the like. Animals can be tagged with a name and a zip code and put on the bulletin board for display. Pin pieces of cut yarn from the top to the bottom of the bulletin board to make it look like a zoo cage.

- Let the children look around the classroom for zeros. If there aren't any, let them write zeros on the chalkboard.

- Let the children practice printing Zs. Point out that a Z has a zigzag shape.

- Let the children play the game Zoom. In a large open area, tell the children to respond to the words you call, such as *crawl, walk, skip, swim, waddle, gallop, tiptoe, crab-walk, inchworm, snake-walk,* and *eggbeater.* On *zoom,* they can run anywhere.

- Help the children write a class letter to someone (they can dictate and you can write). Discuss the importance of zip codes, and include the correct one on the letter.

- Take the class on a field trip to a nearby zoo.

- Show the children pictures of zebras, and point out major parts such as the mane, tail, and hooves. Then let the children paint large pictures of zebras using black and white paints.

- If there is snow on the ground, take the children outside and have them make giant Zs in the snow with their feet. If this is not possible, take paintbrushes and water outdoors. Let the children paint large Zs on the sidewalks or playground with water. Be sure the children use heavy-duty paintbrushes.

COOKING

Zesty Zucchini Bread (requires oven)

3 eggs   1 c. oil   2 c. packed brown sugar
2 c. grated, raw, unpeeled zucchini   3 c. flour   1 t. salt
1 t. baking soda   1 T. vanilla extract   1 c. chopped nuts

Beat the eggs. Add the oil, sugar, and zucchini, and mix well. Stir in the flour, salt, and soda, and fold in the vanilla and nuts. Pour the batter into two greased and floured 5-by-9-inch loaf pans. Bake at 350° F. for one hour. Remove the loaves from the pans and cool them on a rack.

Zingers

1 c. peanut butter   1 c. powdered milk   1 c. honey
1/4 c. wheat germ   a variety of fillings (raisins, chocolate chips, nuts, jam, jelly)

Combine all the ingredients, and mix well. Drop the mixture by tablespoons onto a cookie sheet. Press the cookies into patties about three inches in diameter. Let each child pick a filling and put some in the center of a patty. Have the children close the patty around the filling and roll it into a ball. Chill the Zingers before eating.

Introducing the Vowels

Apple Animal

Use Patterns 1 and 6.

STORY

Two children, Ann and Andy, go for a walk in the woods. They carry along an ax to chop down things that may be in their path. After they have walked for a while, they hear a mysterious sound: "ă ă ă ă ă." They look around, but they do not see anything. They keep hearing the sound and discover finally that it is being made by hundreds of tiny ants. They decide to follow the ants, who lead them to a creature named Apple Animal. Apple Animal talks to the children: "I am Apple Animal. I have magic apples. I want you to have one. My apples are most delicious and magical. Whenever you take a bite, you cannot see a bite missing in the apple—it always stays whole; the more bites you take, the better the apple tastes." Ann and Andy believe what Apple Animal tells them. They thank the creature and take the wonderful apple home.

SONG
(tune of "Pop Goes the Weasel")

Ann and Andy went for a walk.
The ants were saying ă ă.
Then they saw Apple Animal.
A! Magic Apple! (Pronounce "A" as short vowel.)

85

ACTIONS

A!: children squat down during song and jump up on "A!"

ACTIVITIES

- Ask the children to act out the story of Ann and Andy. Each child who isn't a main character can play the part of an ant.
- Let the children be actresses and actors in a simple play like *Goldilocks and the Three Bears.*
- Discuss the word *adventure.* Let the children make up some adventure stories.
- Show the class how to play Hide the *A.* Have one child leave the room while the rest of the children hide a large paper or plastic *A.* Then have the child return. Tell the children to clap louder as the child gets closer to the *A,* and softer as he or she gets further away.
- Draw a capital and small *A* on a sheet of paper for each child. Have the children make pictures out of the letters.
- Help the children make a list of all the animals that have antlers. Take the children to the library if necessary.
- Have the children draw the story of Ann and Andy on a sheet of paper folded into four squares. Let them draw an important part or feature of the story in each square. When they have finished, the children may cut apart their stories and practice putting them in the correct order.
- Make a large apron with a pocket for the bulletin board, and let the children cut out paper *A*s to put in the pocket.
- Play a listening game for *A* words. When the children hear one, tell them to jump up like antelopes. Remember to intersperse other words with the words that begin with *A.*
- Bring in some ants or an ant farm from a pet shop or museum, and let the children observe the ants' actions.

COOKING

Tell this story before you begin cooking:

Once upon a time there was a little girl who loved stars. Each evening she would sit outside and gaze at them in wonder. The girl learned a lot about stars from talking to people and reading books. She would be disappointed when she couldn't see any stars because of clouds. She collected all kinds of objects that were shaped like stars, including cookie cutters, toys, and decorations. These objects were her favorite things. The little girl often cut out paper stars and hung them in the windows of her room.

One day a big storm came, and it rained for a long time. The little girl didn't see the stars for many nights. Then her uncle came for a visit and saw how sad she was. He told her a wonderful secret. He showed her a place where she could always find a beautiful star. He took a bright red apple and cut it across the middle. Together the girl and her uncle opened the apple, and on each half they saw a lovely star! How happy the girl was! She would never feel sad again when the stars weren't out because now she knew a wonderful secret.

Apple Treats

apples　　*water*　　*1 T. lemon juice*　　*1/2 c. brown sugar or honey*

Core and dice one apple for each child. Cook the apples in an electric skillet with a little water and the lemon juice. Cook the mixture until tender, about 15 or 20 minutes. Add the honey, mash or press through a strainer, or eat as is.

Enor Elephant

Use Pattern 1.

STORY

My name is Enor Elephant. I guess I got that name because I'm so enormous! I have enormous ears, enormous eyes and eyelashes, an enormous trunk, and an enormous body! I have so much energy that I do exercises all the time. I am an expert in emergencies. I have saved many animals, including an eel, an elk, and an eagle. I get excited about echos. I go to the edge of the earth and yell "E-E-E-E-E." Then I hear a nice echo. I eat eleven eggs each day so I won't run out of energy.

SONG
(tune of "Are You Sleeping?")

1. Enor, Enor, Enor, Enor,
   Elephant, Elephant.
   Enor is enormous. Terribly enormous.
   Elephant, Elephant.
2. Enor, Enor, Enor, Enor,
   Elephant, Elephant.
   Enor loves to echo. Really loves to echo.
   Elephant, Elephant.

3. Enor, Enor, Enor, Enor,
   Elephant, Elephant.
   Enor saved an eel. Enor saved an eagle
   And an elk, and an elk.
4. Enor, Enor, Enor, Enor,
   Elephant, Elephant.
   Enor loves to eat eggs, really loves to eat eggs.
   Eleven eggs, every day.

ACTIONS

elephant: make trunk with arm
enormous: raise hands high
echo: cup hands around mouth
eel: make swimming motions
eagle: flap arms
elk: make horns above head
eat: pretend to eat

ACTIVITIES

- Have the class do lots of exercises like Enor does. These could include jumping jacks, sit-ups, and running in place.
- Have the children play an Echo Game in a large room or outdoor area. Have one child say something to a child across the room. The other child must immediately repeat the exact words the first child spoke, making an echo.
- Ask the class to find all the things in the room that use electricity. Help the children make a list or chart of the objects on the chalkboard or paper. Together, count how many were found.
- Have the children paint enormous elephants named Enor.
- Teach the children some facts about elephants. Bring in some books with pictures of elephants for the children to look at (public libraries often have picture files available). If possible, play music in which elephants are supposedly moving about ("Baby Elephant Walk" by Henry Mancini). Let the children pretend to be elephants and move to the music.
- Let the children make an Eggy *E*. Make a giant paper *E* and put it up on the wall or on a bulletin board. Have the children cut out several egg shapes and decorate them. Have them draw a capital or small *E* on each egg and then glue the eggs to the large *E*. Each child will need paper, crayons, scissors, and glue.
- Let the children do an experiment: Can a blown-up balloon stick to a wall? Have each child rub a balloon that has been blown up against either

wool clothing or their hair; then have them put the balloons against a wall, where they will stick due to static electricity. The children can also try to get their balloons to stick to each other.

- Have the children make eggshell vases. You will need to save and wash many eggshells for this project. Each child will need several shells, glue, and a juice can for a vase. Have each child crush several eggshells and pour glue over a juice can. Then tell the children to roll their cans in the crushed shells. When the vases are dry they may be sprayed with paint or shellac. This makes a lovely gift for moms and dads.

- Let the children try egg writing. Mix 3 T. alum with 1 c. vinegar, and let each child write an *E* or a word on the shell of a very fresh egg with the mixture, using a small paintbrush. After the eggs have completely dried, boil them in water for 15 minutes. When the children peel their eggs they will see what they wrote on the egg.

- Tell the class some interesting facts about Eskimos.

- Set up an *E* Exhibit. Tell the children to find as many items beginning with *E* (at home and in school) as they can. Display the items and invite another class to view the exhibit.

COOKING

Enor's Eggs

12 eggs   1 c. milk   1 t. salt

Break the eggs into a bowl. Add the milk and mix well, then stir in the salt and mix again. Pour the mixture into an electric skillet and cook until done, stirring or scrambling occasionally.

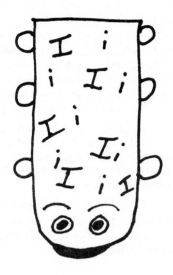

Inky Inchworm

Use Pattern 3.

STORY

My name is Inky Inchworm. I have *I*s all over me. I love the letter *I*. It is so interesting, and it is in so many words. I used to live in an inn, but the conditions there were terrible. Infants cried all the time. Instruments were played, making all kinds of noise. Hundreds of insects lived there too. Now I'm an insect, but I don't like to be so crowded. One day when I couldn't stand the inn another instant, I met an Indian. The Indian listened to my troubles and told me about igloos. Then the Indian and I went to build an igloo. I live there now, and it is wonderful. There are no more interruptions, and there is only one insect.

SONG
(tune of "Old MacDonald Had a Farm")

1. Inky Inchworm lived in an inn.
   I-I-I-I-I.
   And in that inn there were some infants.
   I-I-I-I-I.

With an infant here and an infant there,
Here an infant, there an infant, everywhere an infant.
Inky Inchworm lived in an inn.
I-I-I-I-I.
Other Verses
Substitute *instruments* and *insects* for *infants*.

ACTIONS

inchworm: wiggle up and down
inn: make a roof with hands over head
infants: pretend to hold a baby

Other Actions
instruments: pretend to play a horn
insects: walk fingers up arm

ACTIVITIES

- Have the class dramatize the story of Inky Inchworm. With the exception of Inky, all the children can have parts as infants, insects, or people playing instruments.

- Let the children practice writing their initials. For part of the time during *I* Week, call the children by their initials.

- Let the children make icicles. Give each child a piece of aluminum foil to roll into an "icicle" hanging down. Pin all the icicles to the edges of the bulletin board.

- Discuss with the children what imitating is. Then make sounds, clap patterns, or beat on a drum, and have the children imitate the actions.

- Inflate a balloon for the class, and talk about what is happening. Let each child inflate a balloon. Then think of other things that can be inflated.

- Have the class perform an Indian dance.

- Have the children measure several articles in the room in inches. Let them record their findings on a chart.

- Have the children take part in an ironing project. Have crayon shavings, leaves, and small cut-up pieces of tissue paper available. First, have the children lay some of these items on a sheet of wax paper in an interesting design. Then have the children put another sheet of wax paper over the top and iron the two sheets together. The design will stay in place between the sheets. Let the children round the edges of the wax paper projects or cut them in an interesting way for a nice outer appearance.

COOKING

Ice Cream (noncooked kind for ice cream freezer)

8 eggs   4 c. sugar   4 t. vanilla   2 pt. whipping cream
3-1/2 pt. milk

Beat the eggs slightly, add the sugar, and beat again. Add the cream and beat just until it is well mixed. Add the milk and vanilla and mix well. Pour the mixture into an ice cream freezer, if one is available, and freeze according to directions. Makes one gallon.

An individual freezer for each child's use can be made by using plastic bowls with lids and juice cans. Cut a hole in the lid large enough for the juice can. Pour the ice cream mixture into the juice can, and place the can in the bowl. Pack ice and salt in the bowl around the outside of the juice can. Cover the bowl. Stir the ice cream mixture with a spoon until it hardens. More ice may be added from time to time.

Ice Cream (no ice cream freezer needed)

2 cans sweetened condensed milk   6 T. cocoa   2 c. milk

Mix all the ingredients well, pour into a cake pan, and freeze about three hours. When frozen, cut the ice cream into small squares and serve.

Oh-Oh Octopus

Use Pattern 2.

STORY

My name is Oh-Oh Octopus. I live on the bottom of the ocean.
Everyone calls me "Oh-Oh" because I like to do silly things to make
them laugh. I like to swim around in ovals. My friends call out,
"Oh-Oh!" Then they laugh and laugh: "O-O-O-O-O-O!" I like to hang
on to the oars on someone's boat. My friends call out, "Oh-Oh!" Then
they laugh some more: "O-O-O-O-O-O-O!" They love to watch the
way I eat oranges. They laugh then too: "O-O-O-O-O-O!" I put one in
each of my eight arms and then stick them into my open mouth. I like to
eat oatmeal too. Eating oatmeal under the ocean is hard to do! Can you
think of other silly things that I could do?

SONG
(tune of "The Bear Went over the Mountain")

1. Oh-Oh is an octopus.
   Oh-Oh is an octopus.
   Oh-Oh is an octopus,
   Is an octopus.
2. Oh-Oh swims in the ocean.
   Oh-Oh swims in the ocean.

Oh-Oh swims in the ocean,
In the ocean.

3. Oh-Oh likes to make ovals.
Oh-Oh likes to make ovals.
Oh-Oh likes to make ovals,
To make ovals.

4. Oh-Oh likes to eat oranges.
Oh-Oh likes to eat oranges.
Oh-Oh likes to eat oranges,
To eat oranges.

5. Oh-Oh likes to laugh.
Oh-Oh likes to laugh.
Oh-Oh likes to laugh.
O-O-O-O-O!

ACTIONS

octopus: point four fingers down on each hand to make "pretend" octopus legs
swims: pretend to swim with arm movements
ovals: swing arms in oval pattern
eat: pretend to put things into mouth
laugh: hold sides

ACTIVITIES

- Put together an obstacle course for the children to go through.

- Introduce the word *odor* to the children. Then put various scented things into small jars, and let the children sniff them and try to distinguish what they are.

- Introduce the word *oval* to the children. Then have them try to cut out several paper ovals. An easy way to cut an oval is to begin with a rectangle and cut or round off the corners. When the children can cut ovals well, have them make Oval Owls. Tell the children to glue a small oval to the top of a larger oval to form their animal, and draw in features. If necessary cut ovals for them to use as models.

- Let the children make giant octopuses patterned after Oh-Oh. Have them begin by drawing a body and eight legs on a double thickness of butcher paper. Then have the children cut out the body and legs and staple each together, leaving a hole for stuffing. Have the children stuff each part with crushed newspaper and staple the open area. Then have them staple the legs to the body, sponge-paint the creation, and glue on large eyes and a mouth when the paint has dried. Hang up the octopuses in your classroom for all to see. The class might work together to make one octopus.

- Teach the class some facts about ostriches or otters. Bring in pictures if possible.
- Have the children make an ocean mural, painting lots of different plants and animals that are found in the ocean. Bring in pictures of the ocean floor if the children are not familiar with ocean inhabitants.
- Teach the children to read the words *on* and *off*. Then tell the children to stand up and put a sheet of newspaper on the floor in front of each child. When you flash the word *on* they should get on their paper. When you flash the word *off*, they should step off the paper.

COOKING

Oatmeal

12 c. cold water   3 t. salt   6 c. instant rolled oats
Optional: *raisins, milk, honey*

Put the oats and the salt in the water, bring them to a boil, and cook the mixture for one minute, stirring occasionally. Cover the pan, remove it from the heat, and let it stand for a few minutes. Serve the oatmeal with raisins, milk, and honey.

Oh-Oh's Orange O's

1 orange half   honey   raisins   unsweetened coconut

Provide the above ingredients for each child. Then let each one use some raisins and coconut (or other fruits cut into small chunks) to make an *O* on the orange.

Ugboo

Use Patterns 1 and 10.

STORY

My name is Ugboo. I am from outer space. The name of my planet is UgUgUg. I get to earth on a magic umbrella that takes me anywhere. All I have to do is to say the magic words "Ug a boo, ug a boo, and a boo boo ug a." I often come to Earth to rest in the jungle. Once, when I was resting there under a tree, I heard these little sounds: "ŭ-ŭ-ŭ-ŭ-ŭ-ŭ-ŭ." I opened my eyes and saw lots of little purple creatures called Uglies. The Uglies said, "Ŭ-ŭ-ŭ-ŭ, we want your magic umbrella!" Well, I love my umbrella and didn't want to give it up, so I began trying to trade things. I tried my urn, my unicycle, some delicious upside-down buns, and my ukelele. Each time, the Uglies just shook their heads and said, "Uh-uh, we want your magic umbrella!" Then I thought of something neat we have on UgUgUg. I opened my jug and gave each Ugly a taste of my Unpop. The Uglies loved it. They wanted more. I told them I would bring them lots of Unpop if I could keep my umbrella. They agreed. So on my next trip to Earth I bought the Uglies some Unpop and took them for rides with me on my magic umbrella. (At the end of the story, if you wish, serve each child a little cup of Unpop, which can be any kind of fruit juice.)

97

SONG
(tune of "Michael Row Your Boat Ashore")

1. Ugboo loved his umbrella.
   Ugh, ugh, ugh, ugh.
   Ugboo loved his umbrella.
   Ugh, ugh, ugh, ugh, ugh.
2. Ugboo met the Uglies.
   Ugh, ugh, ugh, ugh.
   Ugboo met the Uglies.
   Ugh, ugh, ugh, ugh, ugh.
3. Ugboo gave them Unpop.
   Ugh, ugh, ugh, ugh.
   Ugboo gave them Unpop.
   Ugh, ugh, ugh, ugh, ugh.
4. Ugboo kept the umbrella.
   Ugh, ugh, ugh, ugh.
   Ugboo kept the umbrella.
   Ugh, ugh, ugh, ugh, ugh.

ACTIONS

umbrella: pretend to hold an umbrella
uglies: make an ugly face
unpop: pretend to drink

ACTIVITIES

- Let the children dramatize the story of Ugboo and the Uglies.
- Have the children jump up, crawl under things, and hang upside-down from a bar for exercising.
- Have the children draw and cut out what they think an Ugly looks like. They can decorate their creatures with glued on items or crayons.

- Ask the children to bring umbrellas to school. Then find a large open area, and let the class open their umbrellas and move to music. Remind the children to keep the sharp umbrella tips away from each other.
- Show the children how to play the Un-game. Give them directions like the following:

tie—untie	snap—unsnap	button—unbutton	zip—unzip
silly—unsilly	do—undo	asleep—unasleep	

- Invite the children to bring an uncle to school for a visit during *U* Week. If some uncles are unavailable, let the children draw their uncles' pictures.
- Have a skilled person come in to play a ukelele for the children.
- Hang up an umbrella in an open area of your room. Have each child cut out a *U*, tie the *U* to a string, and hang the strings under the umbrella.
- Let the children study a map and find where they live in the United States.
- Let those children who wish to tell about a time when they were unhappy.
- Let the children take balls, beanbags, and other safe articles outdoors and practice throwing them *up*.

COOKING

Unpop 1

Large can of pineapple slices with juice
4 c. water   3 T. honey   1 t. ginger

Cut the pineapple into small pieces. Mix all the ingredients well. (Use a blender, if one is available.) Pour into small glasses and enjoy.

Unpop 2

3 c. berries   4 c. milk   3 T. honey

Mix all the ingredients well. (Use a blender, if one is available.) Pour into small glasses and enjoy.

Unpop 3

6 c. milk   1 c. peanut butter   3 T. honey   1 t. cinnamon

Mix all the ingredients well. (Use a blender, if one is available.) Pour into small glasses and enjoy.

Unpop 4

6 c. milk   3 c. orange juice   6 T. honey

Mix all the ingredients well. (Use a blender, if one is available.) Pour into small glasses and enjoy.

Alphabet Week

When you have introduced all the puppets and all the letters of the alphabet, celebrate! Declare an Alphabet Week! Use the week as a time to review letters and sounds, go over old favorites, and play games to reinforce the alphabet.

GROUP AND INDIVIDUALIZED GAMES

Listed below are some games that you can use during Alphabet Week—or anytime. You can use the entire alphabet or a few letters at a time, depending on the needs and abilities of your children. Group games are described first, followed by individualized games.

Group Games

- *Alphabet Soup.* Have the children sit on chairs in a circle. Each child should hold a large card on which a letter of the alphabet is printed. (There should be two of each letter in the game.) Begin the game by standing in the middle of the circle and calling out a letter, perhaps *B*. The two children holding *B* cards must exchange places before you sit in one of their seats. If one of the children does not get to a chair before you do, that child becomes the new caller. A caller may call any letter being used or "Alphabet Soup." If he or she calls "Alphabet Soup," everyone in the circle must find a different chair.

- *Alphabet Tap.* Walk around the children, reciting the alphabet. Stop at random, and tap the child closest to you, who must continue saying the alphabet until he or she stops and taps someone else. When the tapper reaches Z, have the child start over again.

- *Hidden ABCs.* Hide large letters around the room. Then tell the children to go on a hunt, find the letters, and lay them out in the correct order.

- *Doggie Grow.* Play this game with a small group of children. Write the letters of the alphabet on separate cards. Have the children make a two-part dog. One part will represent the dog's head and front legs; the other, its back legs and tail. Have the children take turns naming the letters of the alphabet. When they are successful, they get to make the dog "grow" by moving the tail end and adding to the dog's middle the card marked with the letter they have named.

- *Giant.* Play this game with a small group of children. Have the children sit in a circle. Hold a stack of letter cards and flash one at each child going around the circle. If the child can name the letter, he or she gets to "grow" like a giant. Each stage of growth requires a correct naming of a letter—from a sitting position on the floor to a kneeling position to sitting on a chair to standing on a chair to standing on a chair with hands over head, and, finally, to standing on tiptoes on a chair with hands above head. The first child to become a giant wins. The game can be reversed and called Elf.

- *Magic Two.* Sit in front of the children with one set of capital letters and one set of small letters. Hold up a card from each set. Tell the children to softly call out "Magic" if the cards are the same or match.

- *Elephant.* Print one letter of the alphabet on a paper peanut. If a child knows the letter when you flash it, he or she may feed the peanut letter to the elephant which has been made from paper and set up on a table. Variations could be airplanes landing at an airport or ducks swimming in a pond.

- *Clay Tablets.* Make play-dough from the recipe found in the Activities section of the letter *N*, adding enough water to make it a kneading consistency. Give each child a small amount to be rolled to a thickness of

1/4 to 1/2 inch. Then let each child press a few magnetic or molded letters into the tablet, let them harden, and cut them out.

- *Letter Person.* To the tune of "Muffin Man" have the group sing:
Oh, do you know the Letter Person,
The Letter Person, the Letter Person?
Oh, do you know the Letter Person
That lives on Alphabet Lane?
Choose one child to be the Letter Person, and give him or her a small letter card. Give each of the children a capital letter card. Then have the Letter Person skip around the circle looking for the person with the matching letter. When the proper letter is found, have both children skip around together singing:
Oh, yes, we know the Letter Person,
The Letter Person, the Letter Person.
Oh, yes, we know the Letter Person
That lives on Alphabet Lane.

- *Steal the Bacon.* Divide the class in half, and have each half stand on a goal line opposite the other. Pin a letter to each child—capital letters on the members of one team, small letters on the others. An object, perhaps an eraser, can be the *bacon*, and is placed midway between the two goal lines. Call out a letter and tell both children who wear that letter to race to the bacon. The child who steals the bacon and returns to the goal line with it without being tagged makes a point for the team. If the child is tagged by the person with the partner letter, the other team gets the point.

- *Letter Train.* Have the children sit at their desks or on the floor. Then call out a letter. As each seated child says a word that begins with the letter, tell him or her to get on the train by hooking arms around the waist of the teacher or the last child added to the train. No two children can get on the train by using the same word. Have the train move around making the sound of the letter. After a few moments call, "Train wreck!" and have the children sit down and begin the game again with a new letter.

- *Letter Game.* Let each child make a letter sign with tagboard. Then string yarn through the top of the signs so they can be worn around the neck. Let the children take turns choosing a letter to wear home and have them bring in to class an object in a paper bag that begins with their letter. Have each child give a clue for their object, such as, "It is a toy," and have the rest of the class guess what the object is. Play the game each day until all children have had a turn. (This is a good game to help children to practice their sounds and become more comfortable in front of a group.)

- *Going Fishing.* Make several paper fish, write a letter on each one, and put a few staples in each fish. Then put the fish in a large bucket or basket.

Make a pole out of a pencil and put a magnet at the end of the string. Let each child go fishing, naming something that begins with the letter on the fish he or she catches.

- *Stop, Look, and Listen.* Have all the children stand in a line beside each other. Hold up a letter of the alphabet and say a word. If the word begins with the displayed letter, the children should run to a predetermined goal line. If not, they should stay in place.

- *Shopping at the Supermarket.* Give each child a set of pictures—one for each consonant being studied. Call out a letter as you walk around with a shopping bag. When the children find the picture of an item that begins with the letter called, they should put it in the shopping bag.

Individualized Games

- *Clothespin Match.* Make a gameboard with the capital letters written around the edges. Have the child match clothespins that have small letters on them to the correct capital on the gameboard. The game can be made self-checking by making symbols on the back of the board to match the symbols on the clothespins.

- *Curly Alphabet Game.* Write single capital letters on large plastic curlers and small letters on small curlers. Have the child put together the curlers with the same letter.

- *Parking Lot.* On a gameboard, make parking spaces with a felt-tip marking pen, and print one capital letter in each space. On small toy cars, write or attach a small letter. Then have the child drive the right car into the right parking space.

- *Tongue Game.* Draw a large face on a piece of cardboard, and cut out a big hole for the mouth. On different tongues, write a letter that you are studying. Have the child call out the letter as the face "sticks out its tongue."

- *Piggy Bank Game.* Make a large cardboard pig with a slit in the body. Then attach the pig to one side of a box so the slit is right above the box. Write one letter on each of 26 round pieces of paper that resemble coins. Hold up one coin at a time. Let the child name it and then put it through the slot into the piggy bank box.

- *Jewelry Alphabet.* Write letters on wooden beads of various sizes and colors (you can use a muffin tin or divided box to store the beads). Have the child string the beads on yarn in alphabetical order. Instead of stringing, the child could also sort the beads back into the muffin tin.

- *Order, Order!* Put the starting letter of an object on a cut-out or picture of it. Then have the child put the objects in alphabetical order.

- *Choo-Choo.* Make small cardboard train cars with one alphabet letter on each. Have the child put the train on the "right track" by putting it in alphabetical order.

- *Tapes.* Record several alphabet books for individual children to use at a listening center.

- *Alphabet Pockets.* Sew or glue 26 pockets with one letter on each onto a piece of washable material. Let the child put the correct plastic or paper letter into the correct pocket.

- *Sad Sam.* This game can be played by two or more children or by one child with an aide or helper. First, cut out small paper circles with one letter on each, and draw a sad face on a few of them. Put all the circles in a box. Then tell the child to close his or her eyes and draw out a letter. If the child can name the letter, the circle can be kept; if not, the letter must be put back in the box. If the child gets a sad-faced circle, all the circles collected must go back in the box. You may also wish to include some happy faces; if a child gets one of these, he or she can have an extra turn.

- *Dog and the Bone.* Draw a cardboard dog, several dog dishes, and several bones. Write one letter on each dog dish and each bone, and have the children match them. The bones and dishes can be keyed to make the game self-checking.

- *Zoo Game.* Put letters on plastic tomato or strawberry containers. Then have the child put small plastic animals (found in variety stores) into the "cage" with the correct letter of the animal's beginning sound.

- *Bottlecap Alphabet.* Glue letters inside bottle caps and have the children put the caps in alphabetical order.

- *Post Office.* Write one letter on each of 26 envelopes and put a paper-punch hole in each. Then pin a simple paper house for each letter on the bulletin board. Have the child "mail" the letter to the appropriate house, hanging the letter on the pin. Matching can be for identical letters, capital to small, or letter to sound.

ALPHABET PARTY FOR PARENTS

As part of Alphabet Week, invite the parents into the classroom for an Alphabet Party. The children can help make alphabet pretzels or pancakes (see recipes below) to serve at the party. Parents can join the children in playing individual and group games—perhaps the children's favorite games from those they've played during Alphabet Week. ("Alphabet Soup," found in the Group Games section of Alphabet Week, is an especially good game to play with parents, because everyone gets involved in a fun way.) The children can introduce a few of their favorite puppets by acting out their favorite stories.

Recipes for Alphabet Party

Alphabet Pretzels

3/4 c. water   2 eggs beaten with 2 T. water   1-1/2 pkg. yeast
6 c. flour   1-1/2 T. sugar   1-1/2 t. table salt   kosher salt

Dissolve the yeast in the water. Mix together the flour, sugar, and table salt, and mix into the yeast. Knead. Give each child enough dough to form a letter. When ready, brush each letter with the egg-water mixture. Sprinkle the letters with kosher salt and bake them at 425° F. for 25 minutes. If necessary, store in a tightly covered container.

Alphabet Pancakes

1 c. flour   1 t. baking powder   1/2 t. soda   1/4 t. salt
1 T. oil   1 egg   1 c. liquid (milk, buttermilk, water)
Optional: *butter, syrup, honey*

Mix the ingredients together. Pour the batter onto a hot griddle to form the letters. Serve with butter and syrup or honey. The recipe makes 12–14 small pancakes.

APPENDIX A
A Sample Weekly
Parent Letter

November 19

Dear Mom and Dad,

Hello! After an interesting and exciting week at school we have much to share with you.

Our puppet this week was Wacky Walrus. Wacky is a wonderful, wooly walrus who lives in a wigwam in the wilderness. With Wacky lives a little worm named Wiggly. Wiggly and Wacky whisper all through the day. They both like to waltz, too, and they sing, "Wah, wah, wah, wah."

Our activities with Wacky this week were:

- A waddling relay.
- Making weird witches for art.
- Weaving. (The children will be bringing home their designs.)
- Making wagons out of celery, carrots, toothpicks, and peanut butter.

Wacky's song went to the tune of "Doggie in the Window":

How much is that walrus in the window,
The one with the wiggling worm?
How much is that walrus in the window?
Let's wink now for Wacky Walrus. Wink, wink!

We also waddled, waltzed, and wept, as well as winked. Your child can teach you the actions for the song.

Thank you for all your help in sending *W* materials this week. Wacky's table was very full.

Sincerely,

APPENDIX B
Puppet Patterns
and Directions

Any puppet described in this book can be made by using either one or two of the patterns in this Appendix. The pattern numbers needed to make a particular puppet are given on the page which introduces the letter of the alphabet given in the puppet's initials. Where only one number is given, only a body pattern is required. Where two numbers are given, the first indicates the body pattern to be used, and the second the face pattern needed.

Directions for making the puppets follow:

1. Make an enlarged grid on paper or cardboard, spacing the vertical and horizontal lines to form 1-inch squares. Then copy the pattern, one square at a time, using (if desired) a ruler or compass for accuracy. Cut out the enlarged pattern. Label the pattern with its identifying number for future use. Transfer any additional cutting lines to the enlarged pattern.

2. Pin the body pattern to two thicknesses of material, or trace the pattern on the top piece of material, and cut out the front and back body pieces. To make an opening mouth for Curly Caterpillar, Inky Inchworm, or Spotty Snake, use only the smaller section of Pattern 3 to cut two additional pieces of material (perhaps in a contrasting color). You may wish to use the same pattern piece to cut out Pellon or heavy paper reinforcement pieces. Pin or trace the face pattern onto one thickness of material and cut out the face piece, if one is required. Puppets which need no separate face piece are Curly Caterpillar, Enor Elephant, Goofy Ghost, Inky Inchworm, Jolly Jogger, Noisy Newt, Oh-Oh Octopus, Polka Pig, Quacky Quacker, Spotty Snake, Tricky Turkey, and Wacky Walrus.

3. For all puppets but Curly Caterpillar, Inky Inchworm, and Spotty Snake (if optional mouthpiece is to be used), sew or glue the body front to the body back. The body may be sewn by hand if a machine is not available.

a. If you sew, use strong but flexible thread (polyester or cotton-wrapped polyester, for example). Use one of the following methods:

- Place the two pieces wrong sides together and sew a 1/8- to 1/4-inch seam. Cover with prefolded seam binding which is wide enough to cover seam and stitching. Stitch binding to material, being careful to secure both sides of binding.

- Place the two pieces right sides together and sew a 1/8- to 1/4-inch seam; trim the 1/4-inch seam to 1/8 inch if material is bulky. Clip seam allowance just to the stitching at regular (1/2-inch) intervals around the curves. Do *not* clip stitching. Turn the puppet piece inside out so that wrong sides are together; press seams flat with iron. Sew another line of stitching 1/4 inch from the edge.

b. If you glue the back and front together, put glue on edges of wrong side of back (being sure to leave opening for hand). Place wrong side of puppet's front onto back and press firmly. Allow glue to dry for several hours before using. Glues that work well are Elmer's, Tack, or Bond 527 Multipurpose Cement.

4. To create the optional mouthpiece for Curly Caterpillar, Inky Inchworm, or Spotty Snake, join each reinforced mouthpiece to a body piece, right sides together. Then place the two body pieces right sides together and stitch side seams—but only to mouthpiece opening. Turn the puppet right side out and join the two mouthpieces at the back of the mouth opening to complete the puppet. Reinforce the corners of the mouthpiece joining by hand.

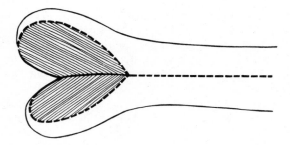

5. You may prefer to attach features and accessories to the body pieces before you join them. Glue and/or iron on additional features and accessories. Iron-on patches can be cut up to make iron-on features. Add additional details—such as freckles or spots—right on the material with a felt-tip pen. Add feathers, buttons, and other decorative items.

PUPPET PATTERN 1

Use for:

Apple Animal
B. B. Bunny
Ditto Dog
Enor Elephant
Friendly Frog
Happy Hippo
Jolly Jogger
Kicky Kangaroo
Looney Lion
Merry Mouse
Noisy Newt
Polka Pig
Quacky Quacker
Racing Raccoon
Ugboo
Vam Vampire
Wacky Walrus
X-Ray X
Yodeling Yak
Zippy Zebra

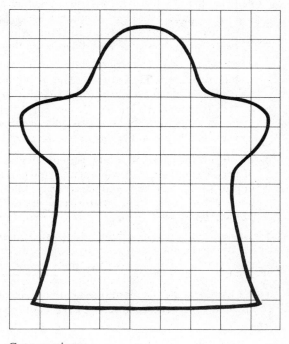

Cut two pieces
1 square = 1 inch

PUPPET PATTERN 2

Use for:

Oh-Oh Octopus

Tricky Turkey

Goofy Ghost

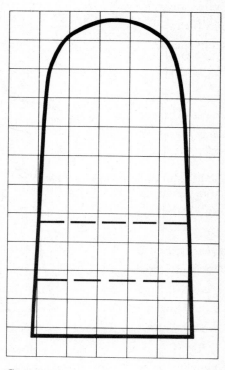

Cut here for Oh-Oh Octopus

Cut here for Tricky Turkey

Cut here for Goofy Ghost

Cut two pieces

1 square = 1 inch

PUPPET PATTERN 3

Use for:

Curly Caterpillar

Inky Inchworm

Spotty Snake

Cut here for optional mouthpiece

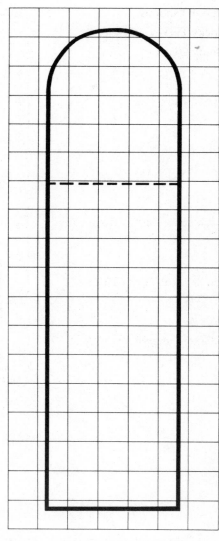

Cut two pieces

1 square = 1 inch

Optional: Cut two *extra* pieces for mouthpiece,
using dashed line as bottom cutting line.
See directions on page 110.

PATTERN 4

Use for:

B. B. Bunny

Merry Mouse

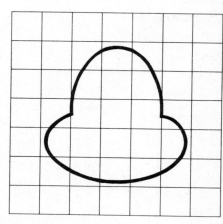

Cut one piece

1 square = 1 inch

PATTERN 5

Use for:

Kicky Kangaroo

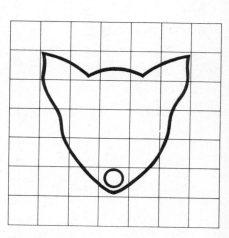

Cut one piece

1 square = 1 inch

PATTERN 6

Use for:

Apple Animal

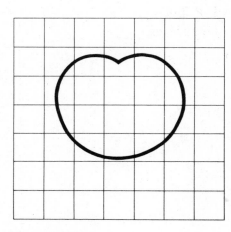

Cut one piece
1 square = 1 inch

PATTERN 7

Use for:

Happy Hippo

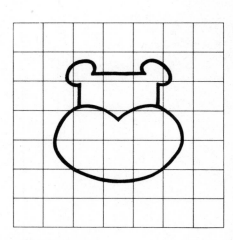

Cut one piece
1 square = 1 inch

PATTERN 8

Use for:

Friendly Frog

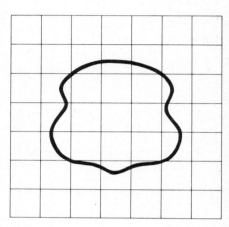

Cut one piece

1 square = 1 inch

PATTERN 9

Use for:

X-Ray X

Racing Raccoon

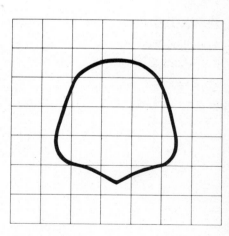

Cut one piece

1 square = 1 inch

PATTERN 10

Use for:
Ditto Dog
Ugboo

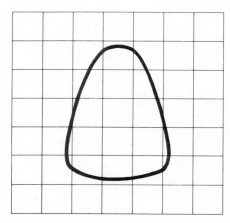

Cut one piece
1 square = 1 inch

PATTERN 11

Use for:
Looney Lion
Yodelling Yak
Zippy Zebra
Vam Vampire

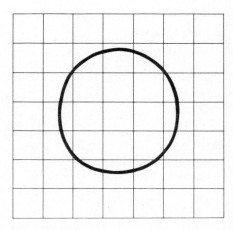

Cut one piece
1 square = 1 inch

APPENDIX C
Writing the Alphabet:
Teaching Letter Formation

Some controversy exists over the question of whether or not children should be taught exact letter formation and if it is taught, when it should be done. If you choose to teach letter formation in your program, have fun while doing it. The children, either individually or in a group, can learn to write in a rhythm that makes the experience much more enjoyable for them—and you!

Following are some directions for teaching letter formation. With them the children learn to write, saying a word or group of words as they do so. A rhythm is produced, promoting smoothness in writing. For example, in the case of a capital *A*, the children say:

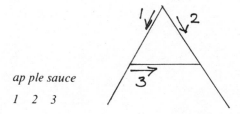

ap ple sauce
1   2   3

When children first learn to write, they have a tendency to expect perfection and therefore spend a great deal of time erasing their letters and trying over and over to get things just right. In this method of rhythm writing, the children have to keep going. Eventually they become more satisfied with their performance as the writing comes more naturally. Be sure the children

119

understand how the letter is formed before they begin to write; then let them practice with the rhythm.

Following is a list of words that you may wish to use as you teach letter formation. But the listed words are by no means the only ones possible. Ordinary nursery rhymes can be used—"Three Blind Mice" for *A*, for example—or any other words that fit the shape of the construction.

Capital letters		*Lower-case letters*	
1. ap- 2. ple- 3. sauce		1. ap- 2. ple	
1. beads 2. buttons 3. bows		1. Bun- 2. ny	
1. Curly		1. Curly	
1. Ditto 2. Dog		1. Ditto 2. Dog	
1. E- 2. nor 3. Ele- 4. phant		1. Ele- 2. phant	
1. Friend- 2. ly 3. Frog		1. Friend- 2. ly	
1. Goofy 2. Ghost		1. Goofy 2. Ghost	
1. Hap- 2. py 3. Hippo		1. Hip- 2. po	

1. Inky
2. is an
3. inchworm

1. inch
2. worm (dot the *i*)

1. Jolly

1. Jol-
2. ly (dot the *j*)

1. Kang-
2. a-
3. roo

1. Kang-
2. a-
3. roo

1. Li-
2. on

1. Lion

1. M (sound)
2. M
3. M
4. M

1. Mer-
2. ry
3. Mouse

1. Noi-
2. sy
3. Newt

1. Nois-
2. y

1. Octopus

1. octopus

1. Pol-
2. ka

1. Pol-
2. ka

1. quack
2. quack

1. Quacky
2. Quacker

1. race
2. race
3. race

1. rac-
2. coon

1. Spotty Snake

1. Spotty Snake

1. Tur-
2. key

1. Tur-
2. key

1. Ugboo

1. umbrel-
2. la

1. Vam-
2. pire

1. Vam-
2. pire

1. Wac-
2. ky
3. Wal-
4. rus

1. Wac-
2. ky
3. Wal-
4. rus

1. X-Ray
2. X

1. X-Ray
2. X

1. Yodel-
2. ing
3. Yak

1. yo-
2. del

1. zip
2. zip
3. zip

1. zip
2. zip
3. zip

Fearon Teacher-Aid Books...
The Idea Books That Free You to Teach

Selected additional titles in *early childhood education:*

COOL COOKING FOR KIDS: Recipes and Nutrition for Preschoolers; P. McClenahan and I. Jaqua. A comprehensive "idea" book on nutrition and cooking techniques for teachers of very small children. Management suggestions, recipes, resources on nutrition, health notes. 9″ × 6″; 176 pages; line art. #1614-X

FREE AND INEXPENSIVE MATERIALS FOR PRESCHOOL AND EARLY CHILDHOOD, Second Edition; Robert Monahan. Over 400 items for early-childhood or primary-grade teacher to obtain free or at little cost. Films, books, pamphlets, posters. 5-1/2″ × 8-1/2″; 126 pages. #3175-0

150 PLUS! GAMES AND ACTIVITIES FOR EARLY CHILDHOOD; Zane Spencer. For any teacher of preschool children; here are over 150 activities for readiness skills, motor skills, and more. All activities are easy to set up and manage. 6″ × 9″; 160 pages; illus. #5068-2

CREATIVE ART FOR THE DEVELOPING CHILD: A Teacher's Handbook; Clare Cherry. A practical manual for conducting art activities that will enhance the young child's perceptual and emotional development. Generously illustrated with photos. 7″ × 10″; 192 pages; illus. #1630-1

POTPOURRI OF PUPPETRY; Enid Bates and Ruth Lowes. An inspirational guide to puppetry in the elementary curriculum with a wide range of suggested materials. How-to illustrations and in-use photos. 6″ × 9″; 64 pages; illus. #5500-5

CREATIVE PLAY FOR THE DEVELOPING CHILD: Early Lifehood Education Through Play; Clare Cherry. A comprehensive illumination of the value of play activities of children in a nursery school setting. Emphasizes physical and intellectual benefits of all forms of play. Delightful photos! 6″ × 9″; 272 pages. #1632-8

COOKING IN THE CLASSROOM; Janet Bruno and Peggy Dakan. Thirty easy recipes for primary grades with questions promoting observation, knowledge of ingredients, measurement skills, safety practices, and lots more. Share the delightful diagrams with the children as the cooking progresses. 9″ × 6″; 72 pages; illus. #1610-7

For a complete Teacher-Aid catalog, write **Fearon Pitman Publishers, Inc.,** 6 Davis Drive, Belmont, California 94002. Or telephone (415) 592-7810.